Oxford Reading Tree

Group Activity Sheets

Book 3 for Stages 6, 7, 8 and 9

Thelma Page and Kay Su

OXFORD
UNIVERSITY PRESS

OXFORD
UNIVERSITY PRESS

Great Clarendon Street, Oxford OX2 6DP

Oxford University Press is a department of the University of Oxford.
It furthers the University's objective of excellence in research,
scholarship, and education by publishing worldwide in

Oxford   New York

Auckland   Cape Town   Dar es Salaam   Hong Kong   Karachi
Kuala Lumpur   Madrid   Melbourne   Mexico City   Nairobi
New Delhi   Shanghai   Taipei   Toronto

With offices in

Argentina   Austria   Brazil   Chile   Czech Republic   France   Greece
Guatemala   Hungary   Italy   Japan   Poland   Portugal   Singapore
South Korea   Switzerland   Thailand   Turkey   Ukraine   Vietnam

Oxford is a registered trade mark of Oxford University Press
in the UK and in certain other countries

British Library Cataloguing in Publication Data

Data available

ISBN-13: 978 0 19 918961 8
ISBN-10: 0 19 918961 7

10 9 8 7

Illustrations by Jan Brychta, cover illustration by Alex Brychta
Printed in the UK by Ashford Press Ltd

Contents

Year 2 Term 3

Stage 8

Introduction

The activities in this book have been planned to meet the requirements of the National Literacy Strategy Framework. Within the Literacy Hour, there is time each day for children to work on individual activities while the teacher reads with a group. These copymasters provide focused individual work to reinforce current class and group teaching objectives. Activities marked Ⓐ will probably need the help of an adult (other than the teacher). Activities marked Ⓘ are intended for the children to manage alone after an initial explanation.

The copymasters build upon and supplement the activities and suggestions provided in the Teacher's Guides. They use the children's involvement with the characters and the stories of the *Oxford Reading Tree* to practise and reinforce the skills and knowledge required by the NLS Framework.

The teaching objectives are taken directly from the National Literacy Strategy Framework document. The yearly and termly expectations are matched to *Oxford Reading Tree* stories as follows:

Year 2 Term 1
Stage 6:
In the Garden   *Land of the Dinosaurs*
Kipper and the Giant   *Robin Hood*
The Outing   *The Treasure Chest*

Year 2 Term 2
Stage 7:
Red Planet   *The Lost Key*
Lost in the Jungle   *The Motorway*
The Broken Roof   *The Bully*

Year 2 Term 3
Stage 8:
The Kidnappers   *The Flying Carpet*
Viking Adventure   *A Day in London*
The Rainbow Machine   *Victorian Adventure*

Stage 9:
Green Island   *The Litter Queen*
Storm Castle   *The Quest*
Superdog   *Survival Adventure*

For each book there are three worksheets, aimed at Word level **W**, Sentence level **S** and Text level **T** teaching objectives. There is also a sheet of notes for each book showing the main learning outcomes, explaining what to do and suggesting further activities for more able children. As the children reach the middle to end of Year 2 you might want to give them the sheets and expect them to read and respond with very little further explanation. The level of difficulty is intended for children of average ability at each Stage. Less able children may need the support of an adult. Alternatively, the teacher could use the sheets as part of his or her guided reading time with a group needing more help.

Coverage and record keeping

Pages 7–14 list the teaching objectives for Year 2 Term 1, Term 2 and Term 3. The bold page numbers show the copymaster appropriate to the objective. The italic page numbers indicate a suggestion for a further activity related to that objective. The remaining columns enable you to keep a record of work covered with a group of up to six children.

Further copymasters

These have been planned to allow for teaching objectives not covered by the story-related sheets. They include general sheets for writing stories or collecting new vocabulary, and suggestions for activities involving poetry and non-fiction. At Stage 6 there is a text extract and suggestions for activities covering a variety of teaching objectives.

Assessment

The assessment pages include checklists of words used at Stages 6–9 of *Oxford Reading Tree* stories. There is also a summary checklist of the words from Appendix List 1 for Years 1 and 2 (pages 124 and 125). Many of the story-linked sheets can be used as assessment of particular teaching objectives if children work unaided.

General notes

- It is vital that the copymasters are selected to reinforce current teaching objectives from shared and guided reading sessions.
- The children should have a clear idea of the purpose of the activity as well as understanding the task.
- At Stages 8 and 9 you can expect most children to read and respond to the instructions without a verbal explanation.
  The work-check face is for children to colour when they have finished and checked their work.
- The copymasters reflect the spiral approach of the NLS Framework in returning to basic teaching objectives to reinforce them before moving on.
- The objectives not covered by the copymasters are those based upon oral work such as reading with expression or role play.

NLS record of achievement for Year 2 Term 1

Word level work — Pages — Names

Word level work	Pages							
Phonics, spelling and vocabulary								
Phonological awareness, phonics and spelling 1 to secure identification, spelling and reading of long vowel digraphs in simple words from Y1T3 (the common spelling patterns for each long vowel phoneme) – Appendix List 3	**16 44**							
2 to revise and extend the reading and spelling of words containing different spellings of the long vowel phonemes from Year 1	15 **44**							
3 the common spelling patterns for the vowel phonemes; *oo (short as in good), ar, oy, ow* (Appendix List 3) to identify the phonemes in speech and writing to blend the phonemes for reading to segment the words into phonemes for spelling	**20 44**							
4 to investigate and classify words with the same sounds but different spellings	19 **24 44**							
Word recognition, graphic knowledge and spelling 5 to read on sight and spell approximately 30 more words from Appendix List 1	31							
6 to read on sight high frequency words likely to occur in graded texts matched to the abilities of reading groups	35 **40**							
7 to use word endings, e.g. s *(plural)*, ed *(past tense)*, ing *(present tense)* to support their reading and spelling	**28 44**							
8 to secure understanding and use of the terms 'vowel' and 'consonant'	**36**							
9 to spell common irregular words from Appendix List 1								
Vocabulary extension 10 new words from reading linked to particular topics, to build individual collections of personal interest or significant words	**41**							
Handwriting 11 to practise handwriting patterns from Year 1	**32**							
12 to begin using and practising the four basic handwriting joins: diagonal joins to letters without ascenders, e.g. *ai, ar, un* horizontal joins to letters without ascenders, e.g. *ou, vi, wi* diagonal joins to letters with ascenders, e.g. *ab, ul, it* horizontal joins to letters with ascenders, e.g. *ol, wh, ot.*	**32**							

Sentence level work

Grammar and punctuation								
Grammatical awareness 1 to use awareness of grammar to decipher new or unfamiliar words, e.g. to predict from the text; to read on, leave a gap and re-read	**17 44**							
2 to find examples, in fiction and non-fiction, of words and phrases that link sentences, e.g. *after, meanwhile, during, before, then, next, after a while*	21							
Sentence construction and punctuation 3 to recognize and take account of commas and exclamation marks when reading aloud with appropriate expression	**25 44**							

		Pages						
4	to re-read own writing for sense and punctuation	**29**						
5	to revise knowledge about other uses of capitalization, e.g. for names, headings, titles, emphasis, and begin to use in own writing	**33**						
6	to use a variety of simple organizational devices, e.g. arrows, lines, boxes, keys, to indicate sequences and relationships.	**37**						

Text level work

Comprehension and composition **Fiction and poetry**								
Reading comprehension								
1	to reinforce and apply their word level skills through shared and guided reading	_15 19_ **44**						
2	to use phonological, contextual, grammatical and graphic knowledge to work out, predict and check the meanings of unfamiliar words and to make sense of what they read								
3	to be aware of the difference between spoken and written language through comparing oral recounts with text; make use of formal story elements in re-telling	**44**						
4	to understand time and sequential relationships in stories, i.e. what happened when	**18** _27_						
5	to identify and discuss reasons for events in stories, linked to plot	**22**						
6	to discuss familiar story themes and link to own experiences, e.g. illness, getting lost, going away	_23_						
7	to learn, re-read and recite favourite poems, taking account of punctuation; to comment on aspects such as word combinations, sound patterns (such as rhymes, alliterative patterns) and forms of presentation								
8	to collect and categorize poems to build class anthologies								
Writing composition								
9	through shared and guided reading to apply phonological, graphic knowledge and sight vocabulary to spell words accurately								
10	to use story structure to write about own experience in same/similar form	**26**						
11	to use language of time (see sentence level work) to structure a sequence of events, e.g. 'when I had finished . . . ', 'suddenly . . . ', 'after that . . . '	**30 44**						
12	to use simple poetry structures and to substitute own ideas, write new lines	**42**						
Non-fiction **Reading comprehension**								
13	to read simple instructions in the classroom, simple recipes, plans, instructions for constructing something								
14	to note key structural features, e.g. clear statement of purpose at start, sequential steps set out in a list, direct language								
Writing composition								
15	to write simple instructions, e.g. getting to school, playing a game	_35_ **34**						

	Pages		Names					
16 to use models from reading to organize instructions sequentially, e.g. listing points in order, each point depending on the previous one, numbering								
17 to use diagrams in instructions, e.g. drawing and labelling diagrams as part of a set of instructions	31							
18 to use appropriate register in writing instructions, i.e. direct, impersonal, building on texts read.	38							

NLS record of achievement for Year 2 Term 2

Word level work

Phonics, spelling and vocabulary								
Phonological awareness, phonics and spelling 1 to secure the reading and spelling of words containing different spellings of the long vowel phonemes from Year 1								
2 the common spelling patterns for the vowel phonemes: *air, or, er* (Appendix List 3): to identify the phonemes in speech and writing to blend the phonemes for reading to segment the words into phonemes for spelling	**46**							
3 to read and spell words containing the digraph *wh, ph, ch* (as in *Christopher*)	**70**							
4 to split familiar oral and written compound words into their component parts, e.g. *himself, handbag, milkman, pancake, teaspoon*	**50**							
5 to discriminate orally, syllables in multi-syllabic words using children's names and words from their reading, e.g. *dinosaur, family, dinner, children*. Extend to written forms and note syllable boundaries in speech and writing	**54**							
Word recognition, graphic knowledge and spelling 6 to read on sight and spell all the words from Appendix List 1	61							
7 for guided reading, to read on sight high frequency words likely to occur in graded texts matched to the abilities of reading groups	**71**							
8 to spell words with common prefixes, e.g. *un, dis,* to indicate the negative	**58**							
9 to spell common irregular words from Appendix List 1								
Vocabulary extension 10 new words from reading linked to particular topics, to build individual collections of personal interest or significant words								
11 the use of antonyms; collect, discuss differences of meaning and their spelling	**62**							
Handwriting 12 to practise handwriting patterns from Year 1								
13 to practise handwriting in conjunction with the phonic and spelling patterns above	65							

	Pages	Names					

	Pages						
14 to use and practise the four basic handwriting joins: diagonal joins to letters without ascenders, e.g. *ai, ar, un* horizontal joins to letters without ascenders, e.g. *ou, vi, wi* diagonal joins to letters with ascenders, e.g. *ab, ul, it* horizontal joins to letters with ascenders, e.g. *ol, wh, ot*.	**66**						

Sentence level work

Grammar and punctuation							
Grammatical awareness 1 to use awareness of grammar to decipher new or unfamiliar words, e.g. to predict from the text; to read on, leave a gap and re-read							
2 to read aloud with intonation and expression appropriate to the grammar and punctuation (sentences, speech marks, exclamation marks)							
3 to re-read own writing for grammatical sense (coherence) and accuracy (agreement) – identify errors and suggest alternative constructions							
4 to be aware of the need for grammatical agreement in speech and writing, matching verbs to nouns/pronouns correctly, e.g. *I am, the children are*	65 **47**						
5 to use verb tenses with increasing accuracy in speaking and writing, e.g. *catch/caught, see/saw, go/went* and to use the past tense consistently for narration	**51**						
Sentence construction and punctuation 6 to identify speech marks in writing, understand their purpose, use the term correctly	57 **55**						
7 to investigate and recognize a range of other ways of presenting texts, e.g. speech bubbles, enlarged, bold or italicized print, captions, headings and sub-headings	45 **59**						
8 to use commas to separate items in a list	**63**						
9 to secure the use of simple sentences in own writing.	57 **67**						

Text level work

Comprehension and composition **Fiction and poetry**							
Reading comprehension 1 to reinforce and apply their word level skills through shared and guided reading							
2 to use phonological, contextual, grammatical and graphic knowledge to work out, predict and check the meanings of unfamiliar words and to make sense of what they read							
3 to discuss and compare story themes	**48**						
4 to predict story endings/incidents, e.g. from unfinished extracts while reading with the teacher							
5 to discuss story settings: to compare differences; to locate key words and phrases in texts; to consider how different settings influence events and behaviour	**52**						
6 to identify and describe characters, expressing own views and using words and phrases from texts	**56**						
7 to prepare and re-tell stories individually and through role-play in groups, using dialogue and narrative from text							

	Pages	Names						
8 to read own poems aloud								
9 to identify and discuss patterns of rhythm and rhyme and other features of sound in different poems								
10 to comment on and recognize when the reading aloud of a poem makes sense and is effective								
11 to identify and discuss favourite poems and poets, using appropriate terms (poet, poem, verse, rhyme, etc.) and referring to the language of poems								
Writing composition 12 through shared and guided reading to apply phonological, graphic knowledge and sight vocabulary to spell words accurately	*57*							
13 to use story settings from reading, e.g. re-describe, use in own writing, write a different story in the same setting	**60**							
14 to write character profiles, e.g. simple descriptions, posters, passports, using key words and phrases that describe or are spoken by characters in the text	**68**							
15 to use structures from poems as a basis for writing, by extending or substituting elements, inventing own lines, verses; to make class collections, illustrate with captions, to write own poems from initial jottings and words	**72**							
Non-fiction								
Reading comprehension 16 to use dictionaries and glossaries to locate words by using initial letter	*69* **64**							
17 that dictionaries and glossaries give definitions and explanations; discuss what definitions are, explore some simple definitions in dictionaries	*61* **73**							
18 to use other alphabetically ordered texts, e.g. indexes, directories, listings, registers; to discuss how they are used	**74**							
19 to read flow charts and cyclical diagrams that explain a process								
Writing composition 20 to make class dictionaries and glossaries of special interest words, giving explanations and definitions, e.g. linked to topics, derived from stories, poems								
21 to produce simple flow charts or diagrams that explain a process.								

NLS record of achievement for Year 2 Term 3

Word level work

Phonics, spelling and vocabulary								
Phonological awareness, phonics and spelling 1 to secure phonemic spellings from previous 5 terms	*91 119* **116 120**							
2 to reinforce work on discriminating syllables in reading and spelling from previous term	**80 112**							
3 discriminate, read and spell the phonemes *ear* (hear) and *ea* (head)	**92**							

	Pages	Names						

Word recognition, graphic knowledge and spelling

	Pages							
Word recognition, graphic knowledge and spelling 4 to secure reading and spelling of all the words from Appendix List 1	**96 124 125**							
5 for guided reading, to read on sight high frequency words likely to occur in graded texts matched to the abilities of reading groups	**126 127**							
6 to investigate words which have the same spelling patterns but different sounds	**84 108**							
7 to spell words with common suffixes, e.g. *ful, ly*	*99* **88 100**							
8 to spell common irregular words from Appendix List 1								
Vocabulary extension 9 new words from reading linked to particular topics, to build individual collections of personal interest or significant words	*115*							
10 to use synonyms or other alternative words/phrases that express same or similar meanings; to collect, discuss shades of meaning and use to extend and enhance writing	**76 104**							
Handwriting 11 to practise handwriting in conjunction with the phonic and spelling patterns above								
12 to use the four basic handwriting joins from previous two terms with confidence, and use these in independent writing: diagonal joins to letters without ascenders, e.g. *ai, ar, un* horizontal joins to letters without ascenders, e.g. *ou, vi, wi* diagonal joins to letters with ascenders, e.g. *ab, ul, it* horizontal joins to letters with ascenders, e.g. *ol, wh, ot.*								

Sentence level work

Grammar and punctuation								
Grammatical awareness 1 to read text aloud with intonation and expression appropriate to the grammar and punctuation								
2 the need for grammatical agreement, matching verbs to nouns/pronouns, e.g. *I am, the children are;* using simple gender forms, e.g. *his/her* correctly	**89 113 121**							
3 to use standard forms of verbs in speaking and writing, e.g. *catch/caught, see/saw, go/went* and to use the past tense consistently for narration	**81 105**							
Sentence construction and punctuation 4 to use commas in lists	**97 117**							
5 to write in clear sentences using capital letters and full stops accurately	*115 119* **85 109**							
6 to turn statements into questions, learning a wide range of *wh* words typically used to open questions: *what, where, when, who* and to add question marks	**77 101**							
7 to compare a variety of forms of questions from texts, e.g. asking for help, asking the time, asking someone to be quiet.	**93**							

	Pages	**Names**					

Text level work

	Pages						
Comprehension and composition **Fiction and poetry**							
Reading comprehension							
1 to reinforce and apply their word level skills through shared and guided reading							
2 to use phonological, contextual, grammatical and graphic knowledge to work out, predict and check the meanings of unfamiliar words and to make sense of what they read	**90**						
3 to notice the difference between spoken and written language through re-telling known stories; compare oral versions with the written text							
4 to compare books by the same author; settings, characters, themes, to evaluate and form preferences, giving reasons	95 **98**						
5 to read about authors from information on book covers, e.g. other books written, whether author is alive or dead, publisher; to become aware of authorship and publication							
6 to read, respond imaginatively, recommend and collect examples of humorous stories, extracts, poems	**86**						
7 to compare books by different authors on similar themes; to evaluate, giving reasons							
8 to discuss meanings of words and phrases that create humour, and sound effects in poetry, e.g. nonsense rhymes, tongue twisters, riddles and to classify poems into simple types; to make class anthologies							
Writing composition 9 through shared and guided reading to apply phonological, graphic knowledge and sight vocabulary to spell words accurately	83 91 99						
10 to write sustained stories, using their knowledge of story elements: narrative, settings, characterization, dialogue and the language of story	**94 114** **118 128**						
11 to use humorous verse as a structure for children to write their own by adaptation, mimicry or substitution; to invent own riddles, language puzzles, jokes, nonsense sentences, etc., derived from reading; write tongue twisters or alliterative sentences; select words with care, re-reading and listening to the effect	103 **82 102** **106**						
12 to write simple evaluations of books read and discussed, giving reasons	**110**						
Non-fiction							
Reading comprehension 13 to understand the distinction between fact and fiction; to use the terms 'fact' and 'fiction' and 'non-fiction' appropriately	**78 122**						
14 to pose questions and record these in writing, prior to reading non-fiction to find answers							
15 to use a contents page and index to find way about text							
16 to scan a text to find specific sections, e.g. key words or phrases, subheadings							
17 to skim-read title, contents page, illustrations, chapter headings and sub-headings, to speculate what a book might be about							

	Pages	Names					
18 to evaluate the usefulness of a text for its purpose							
Writing composition 19 to make simple notes from non-fiction texts, e.g. key words and phrases, page references, headings, to use in subsequent writing							
20 to write non-fiction texts, using texts read as models for own writing, e.g. use of headings, sub-headings, captions							
21 to write non-chronological reports based on structure of known texts, e.g. *There are two sorts of x . . . ; They live in x . . . ; the As have x . . . ; but the Bs, etc.* Using appropriate language to present, sequence and categorize ideas.							

Main learning outcome: to secure identification, spelling and reading of long vowel digraphs in simple words (W1)

Further outcome: to revise and extend the reading and spelling of words containing different spellings of the long vowel phonemes (W2)

Activity: Ask the children to read the sentences, and for each sentence to find the word that has the same sound and spelling pattern as the word in brackets. The children put a ring round the word. Then the children spell the words to match the pictures, using the spelling patterns above to help them.

Further activity: Children could write one of the sets of spelling patterns on the back of the sheet, e.g. 'name', 'play' and 'train', and look for further words containing each pattern in their reading book or a picture dictionary. They can list the words in their appropriate groups.

Main learning outcome: to use awareness of grammar to decipher new or unfamiliar words (S1)

Activity: Ask the children to read the sentences and then choose a word from the strawberries to write on the line to complete each sentence. Children should work out the missing words without referring to the text.

Further activity: Children could be given an appropriate number of words from the strawberries to put into simple sentences. They could write the sentences on the back of the sheet.

Main learning outcome: to understand time and sequential relationships in stories (T4)

Further outcome: to reinforce and apply their word level skills through guided reading (T1)

Activity: Ask the children to read the sentences and number them in the order they appear in the story. (The order is 5, 7, 2, 8, 6, 3, 1, 4.) The children then choose the three sentences which tell them what happened first, next and last, and write them on the lines. They draw a picture to match the sentence.

Further activity: Children could choose one of the sentences from the middle of the story to write on the back of the sheet. They look in the book and find a sentence which describes what happened next and write it, starting the sentence with 'Next . . . '.

Read the sentences. In each sentence put a ring round the word with the same sound and spelling pattern as the word in brackets.

The children came out of the jungle. (name)
'Go away, cat,' shouted Kipper. (play)
It began to rain. (train)

'I can't see,' said Chip. (feet)
The children ran to eat them. (seat)
'I feel sick now,' said Kipper. (feet)

The grass was like a jungle. (bite)
We can ride down to the desert. (bite)
Kipper was frightened. (high)

The key began to glow. (show)
'I don't know,' he said. (show)

Kipper went into Chip's room. (moon)
It was too late. (moon)

Spell the words to match these pictures.

_____ _____ _____

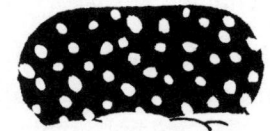

_____ _____ _____

Work
check

All these sentences have the last word missing.

Choose a word from the strawberries to complete the sentences.

'Let's get out of here,' he _____ .

Chip saw a _____ .

Everyone felt _____ .

They were playing in the _____ .

The children got smaller and _____ .

Chip began to _____ .

Let's get inside and ride _____ .

The children climbed _____ .

hot   climb   bumble-bee   down

out   smaller   called   sandpit

Work check

Read the sentences. Number them in the order they appear in the story.

- [ ] The children climbed inside a bottle.
- [ ] The children ate the strawberries.
- [ ] The children were in the grass.
- [ ] Dad looked at his strawberries.
- [ ] Floppy chased the cat away.
- [ ] They came to a mountain.
- [ ] Kipper went into Chip's room.
- [ ] The car took them down the mountain.

Choose three sentences to say what happened **first, next** and **last.**

Write the sentences and draw a picture to match.

| | First .... |
| | .... |

| | Next .... |
| | .... |

| | Last .... |
| | .... |

Work
check

Main learning outcome: the common spelling patterns for the vowel phonemes *oo, ar, oy, ow* (W3)

Further outcome: to investigate and classify words with the same sounds but different spellings (W4)

Activity: Ask the children to read the sentences and put a ring round the word with the same sound and spelling pattern as the word in brackets. The children then read the words and write them on the lines in the pictures beneath the words with the same spelling pattern. Ask the children to spell the words to match the pictures, using the spelling patterns given.

Further activity: Children could write one of the spelling patterns on the back of the sheet e.g. 'car', and look for further words containing that pattern in their reading book or a picture dictionary and list them beneath the word/s.

Main learning outcome: to find examples of words and phrases that link sentences (S2)

Activity: Ask the children to read the words and phrases which are falling out of the giant's case. The children read the sentences and write the word or phrase which best links the sentences on the lines. The children then make up an end to the sentence about Biff and Chip. (If children need help at this point, they could look at pages 4 and 5 which tell them where Biff and Chip were.)

Further activity: Children could complete the sentence 'During the day I . . .' and write and illustrate it on the back of the sheet.

Main learning outcome: to identify and discuss reasons for events in stories, linked to plot (T5)

Further outcome: to reinforce and apply their word level skills through guided reading (T1)

Activity: Ask the children to read the questions and underline the correct reasons for the events. Children then write the answer to why the people had a party.

Further activity: Children could choose another event from the story and, on the back of the sheet, write the reason for its happening.

Read the sentences. In each sentence put a ring round the word with the same sound and spelling pattern as the word in brackets.

He put back the broken roofs. (pull)

You look like a giant. (book)

Let's have a party. (car)

It pointed to the village. (boil)

I'm a boy. (toy)

It's time for me to go now. (cow)

'Stop it,' shouted Kipper. (cloud)

Read these words. Write the words with the same spelling pattern on the pictures.

houses   shook   out   good   ouch   round   took

goodbye   mountain   down   whoosh   pushed

cloud   book   cow   pull

Spell the words to match these pictures.

  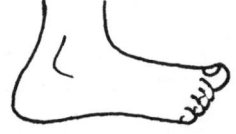

_____   _____   _____

Work check

Read the words that have fallen out of the giant's case. Help the giant find the right words to link the sentences. Write the words on the lines.

Kipper saw a signpost. _____ he came to the village.

The people said, 'Well, you look like a giant.' _____ Kipper began to cry.

Kipper put back the broken roofs. _____ he picked up the stone and put it outside the village.

The village band played for Kipper _____ the giant came back.

'Ouch!' he yelled _____ he fell over the stone.

Make up an end to the unfinished sentence.

Kipper had a giant adventure. Meanwhile, Biff and Chip

_____

_____

Work check

Underline the right answer to each question.

Why did Kipper run to get Biff?
    a) because he fell over a stone.
    b) because the key began to glow.

Why did Kipper go to the village?
    a) because he did not want to meet the giant.
    b) because he wanted to see some little houses.

Why did Kipper begin to cry?
    a) because Biff was out with Chip.
    b) because the people threw things at Kipper.

Why did everyone say, 'Good old Kipper'?
    a) because Kipper helped to mend the houses.
    b) because Kipper put the pig outside the village.

Why was the giant very angry?
    a) because his socks fell out of the case.
    b) because he saw Kipper in the village.

Finish this sentence.

The people shouted, 'Hooray! Let's have a party,'
because _____

Work check

Main learning outcome: to investigate and classify words with the same sounds but different spellings (W4)

Activity: Ask the children to read the pairs of sentences and in each pair to find the two words which sound the same but have different spellings. The children write the words in the boxes. (For some children you may wish to underline one of the words in each pair of sentences.) The children then read the single sentences and choose the correct spelling ('to', 'too' or 'two') to write on the lines.

Further activity: Children could think of their own sentences using the different spellings ('to', 'too' or 'two') and write them on the back of the sheet.

Main learning outcome: to recognize and take account of commas and exclamation marks in reading aloud with appropriate expression (S3)

Activity: Ask the children to read the first four sentences and ring the commas and exclamation marks with the appropriate coloured pencil. The children take turns in reading the pairs of sentences aloud, the adult making sure that the appropriate expression is used. The children then write the missing commas or exclamation marks in the last five sentences.

Further activity: Children could find other sentences in the book using commas or exclamation marks and write them on the back of the sheet.

Main learning outcome: to use story structure to write about own experience in same/similar form (T10)

Further outcome: to discuss familiar story themes and link to own experiences (T6)

Activity: Ask the children to read the simplified story. The children then think of an outing they have been on and write about it, using the sentence structures given where appropriate. (Children who have not been on a school outing could write about an outing from home.)

Further activity: Children could write 'I have been to . . .' on the back of the sheet and list the places they have had outings to, adding any of their own. Children could illustrate their outing on the back of the sheet.

In each pair of sentences there are two words which sound the same but have different spellings. Find the words and write them in the boxes.

'I know what that is called,' said Nadim.

'Oh no!' said Mrs May.

Nadim wanted to see the elephants.

'Can we go to the sea?' said Kipper.

It rained so the children got on the bus.

Mum had to sew Biff's name on.

'Lots of dinosaurs are here,' said Wilf.

Mrs May could hear the children.

Some children looked at the water.

'I can do this sum,' said Wilma.

'It's time for an adventure,' said Biff.

There were four children in the shop.

These sentences have some words missing. Choose **to, two** or **too** and write the correct spelling on the lines.

The children went _____ the zoo.

Wilf got _____ books from the shop.

Wilma went _____ the shop _____ .

_____ and _____ make four.

Work
check

Read these sentences. Put a red ring round the commas.

Put a blue ring round the exclamation marks.

'This is fun,' shouted Nadim.

'Hooray!' shouted the children.

'Don't run away,' said Mrs May.

'Oh Wilf!' said Biff.

Now read these pairs of sentences aloud.

Think about the difference the commas and exclamation marks make.

'What a silly thing to do,' said Mrs May.

'What a silly thing to do!' said Mrs May.

'What a good idea,' said Mrs May.

'What a good idea!' said Mrs May.

'Good, Nadim,' said Mrs May.

'Good Nadim!' said Mrs May.

Write the missing punctuation on the lines in these sentences.

'Oh no ___ ' said Biff.

'This is good ___ ' said Nadim.

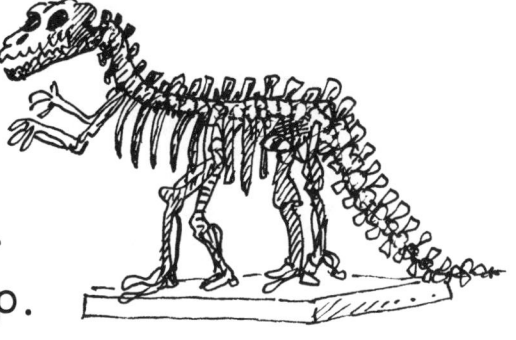

'Ouch ___ ' he yelled.

'I like dinosaurs ___ ' said Nadim.

'Come to our house ___ ' said Chip.

Splash ___ Wilf's shoe landed in the water.

Work
check

Read this story.

The children went on an outing.
A bus took them to a museum.
The children saw lots of dinosaurs.
A lady talked about the dinosaurs.
The children went to the shop.
The bus took the children back to school.
It was time to go home.

Here are some places you may have been on an outing to.

farm   museum   zoo   castle

Write a story about an outing. Use the story above to help you.

....

....

....

....

....

....

Work
check

Main learning outcome: to use word endings *s, ed, ing* to support their reading and spelling (W7)

Activity: Ask the children to read the words, making sure they pronounce the final *s*, and match them to the correct picture. The children read the sentences and write the words ending in *ed* in the eggs. Then the children re-write the words in the eggs changing the *ed* ending to *ing* and put them in the correct sentences. Finally, ask them to read the new sentences they have made.

Further activity: Children could write the endings on the back of the sheet and then make lists of other words in the book with those endings.

Main learning outcome: to re-read own writing for sense and punctuation (S4)

Activity: Ask the children to write their own sentences about the pictures. The children re-read their sentences to check the sense and punctuation. Give the children a correct model sentence if their sentence does not make sense. The children then answer the two questions about their sentences.

Further activity: Children could choose their favourite part of the story and write a sentence about it on the back of the sheet.

Main learning outcome: to use language of time to structure a sequence of events (T11)

Further outcome: to understand time and sequential relationships in stories (T4)

Activity: Ask the children to read the words in the footprints. Then the children read the sentences and write them in the correct order (referring to the book where necessary), starting each sentence with one of the words in the footprints. The starting words can be used in various orders providing 'First' is at the top and the others are used appropriately.

Further activity: Children could write 'In the end' on the back of the sheet and continue to write a suitable sentence.

Match these words to the right pictures.

key   keys   egg   eggs   dinosaur   dinosaurs

Read these sentences.

Biff picked up a stick.

'Go away!' Biff yelled.

'Come up here,' Wilf called.

The dinosaur looked round at Wilf.

Wilf jumped down.

Write the words ending in **ed** in the eggs.

Now change the **ed** ending to **ing** and write the words you have made in the correct spaces. Read the new sentences.

Biff is ——————— up a stick.

'Go away!' Biff is ——————— .

'Come up here,' Wilf is ——————— .

The dinosaur is ——————— round at Wilf.

Wilf is ——————— down.

Work check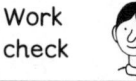

Write a sentence about each picture.

_____

_____

_____

_____

Read your sentences carefully.

Did you remember the capital letters and full stops? Yes / No

Do your sentences make sense? Yes / No

Work
check

Look at these words for starting sentences.

Immediately   First   After that

Meanwhile   Next

Suddenly   Then

Read these sentences.

A dinosaur flew down.
Nadim found some eggs.
Chip found a footprint.
Wilf ran on and climbed a hill.
Biff took a photograph.
A little dinosaur came out of the egg.
Biff picked up a stick.

Write them in the correct order on the lines, starting each sentence with one of the words or groups of words in the footprints.

1 _____

2 _____

3 _____

4 _____

5 _____

6 _____

7 _____

Check your capital letters and full stops.

Work check

Main learning outcome: to practise handwriting patterns (W11); to begin using the four basic handwriting joins (W12)

Further outcome: to read on sight and spell words from Appendix List 1 (W5)

Activity: Ask the children to copy the handwriting patterns, making sure they write between the central lines and take the ascenders up to the dotted line. The children then read the next set of words and copy them in their best handwriting, leaving a space between each word.

Further activity: Children could write their name or 'Robin Hood' on the back of the sheet and choose two or three consecutive letters from the name and design their own writing pattern/s.

Main learning outcome: to revise knowledge about other uses of capitalization, and begin to use in own writing (T5)

Activity: Ask the children to look at page 1 of *Robin Hood* and find the words in capital letters. The children make a list of them on the lines. The children then read the sentence with the capital letters missing, and write it correctly below. They complete the sentences about themselves, using capital letters where appropriate.

Further activity: Children could look for notices or labels around the room written in capital letters and write them on the back of the sheet. They could find notices in other *Oxford Reading Tree* books and write them on the back of the sheet.

Main learning outcome: to write simple instructions (T15)

Further outcome: to use diagrams in instructions (T17)

Activity: Ask the children to look at the pictures and write the instructions as if they were telling Kipper what to do, e.g. 'Hide in the big black pot.'

Further activity: Children could turn to the last page and write on the back of the sheet 'How to make Kipper say "Aaaaaah!" ' followed by the instruction (Sing a song about Robin Hood).

Robin Hood is teaching his men how to write. Write these patterns too.

ololol

ovovov

acacac

illill

Copy these words in your best handwriting.

old

over

can

will

Did you leave a space between each word?

Work
check

Capital letters can be used to make something stand out.

Look at page 1 of <u>Robin Hood</u>.

Make a list of the words that are written in capital letters.

Names always start with a capital letter.

Something is wrong with this sentence. Write it again correctly.

biff, wilma and anneena went to a pantomime about robin hood.

_____

_____

Finish these sentences.

My name is _____

I go to _____ School.

My teacher's name is _____

My friend's name is _____

Work check

Write the instructions for Kipper.

How to rescue Robin Hood and his friends

1

2

....

....

3

4

....

....

5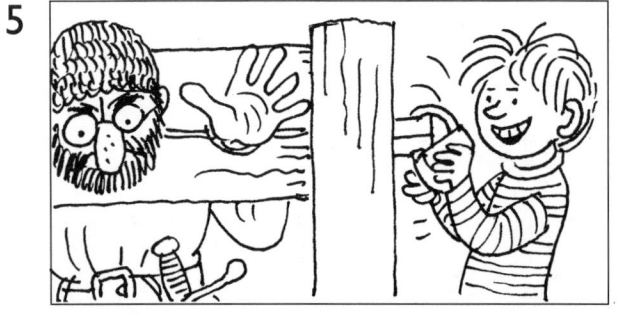

6

....

....

Work
check

Main learning outcome: to secure understanding and use of the terms 'vowel' and 'consonant' (W8)

Further outcome: to read on sight high frequency words likely to occur in graded texts (W6)

Activity: Ask the children to read the alphabet and put a ring round the five vowels. The children then read the words and write them on the octopus if they begin with a vowel, and on the fish if they begin with a consonant. Ask the children to look in the book and find some words to match the vowel/consonant patterns given. They write the words in the boxes.

Further activity: Children could write their name on the back of the sheet and put a ring round the vowels. They could make two lists of names of children in the class, one list of names beginning with a vowel, the other with a consonant.

Main learning outcome: to use simple organizational devices to indicate sequences and relationships (S6)

Activity: Ask the children to read the sentences in the boxes and draw arrows starting at the first sentence and joining them in the right order. The children turn to page 20 in the book and fill in the colour key for Wilma's swimming outfit. They colour the picture using the key.

Further activity: Children could draw a picture of a fish on the back of the sheet and devise a colour key for the picture.

Main learning outcome: to use appropriate register in writing instructions (T18)

Further outcome: to write simple instructions (T15)

Activity: Ask the children to fill in the swimming certificate to say what the children had to do to pass the test. This will take the form of instructions, i.e. jump in the pool, swim ten lengths, swim to the bottom of the pool, pick up a brick, swim with it to the top. The children fill in the names as asked.

Further activity: Children who go swimming could write the instructions they are given on the back of the sheet. Children could list general classroom instructions on the back of the sheet.

Read the alphabet and put a ring round the 5 vowels.

a b c d e f g h i j k l m n o p q r s t u v w x y z

Read these words from <u>The Treasure Chest</u>.

Write the words that begin with a vowel on the octopus.

Write the words that begin with a consonant on the fish.

every   children   were   air   said   old   pool   up   gold

down   test   it   very   about   look   big   magic   under

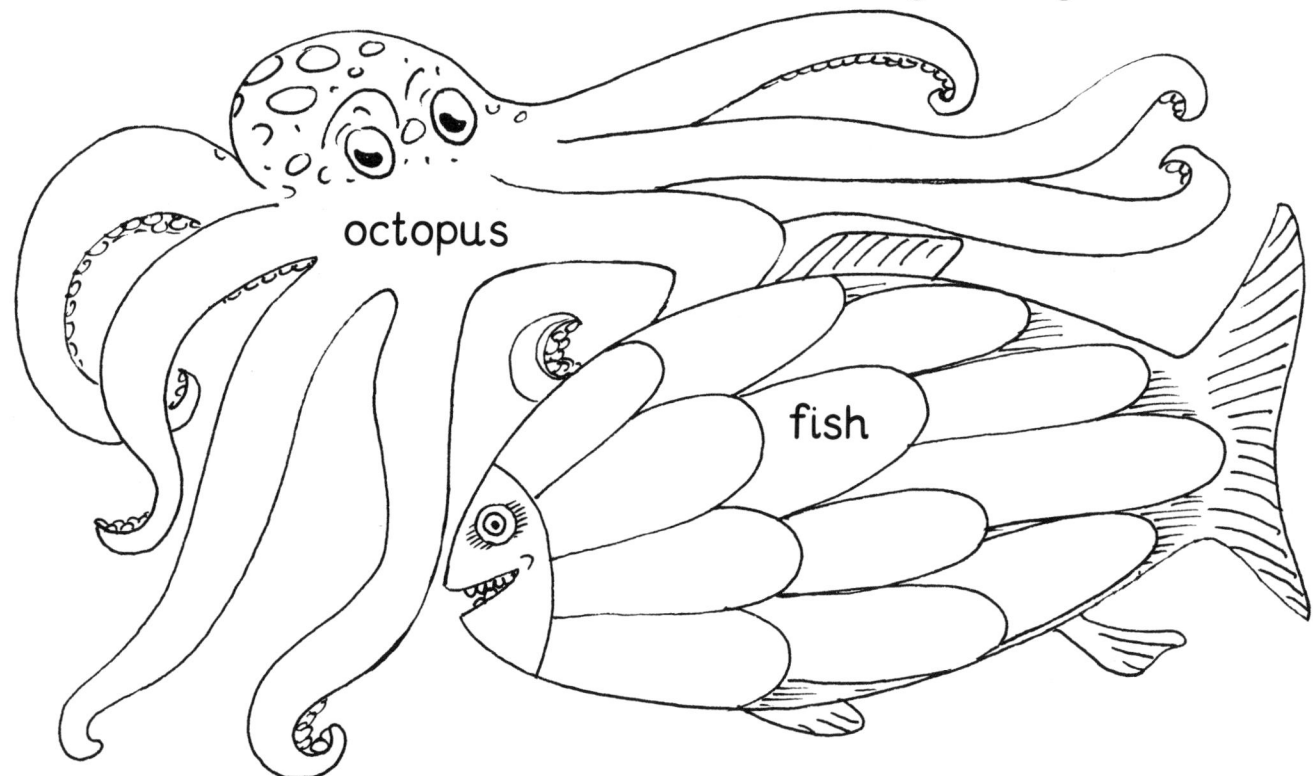

octopus

fish

Find some words in the book that follow these patterns.

c = consonant   v = vowel

v	c

c	v

c	v	c

c	c	v

c	v	v	c

c	c	v	c

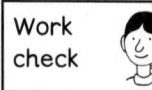

Work
check

Draw arrows to join the sentences in the right order.

The magic began to work.	They saw an octopus sitting on a chest.
They swam up to the ship.	The children could swim underwater.
They saw a ship under the water.	The octopus swam away.
It was full of gold.	The children opened the chest.

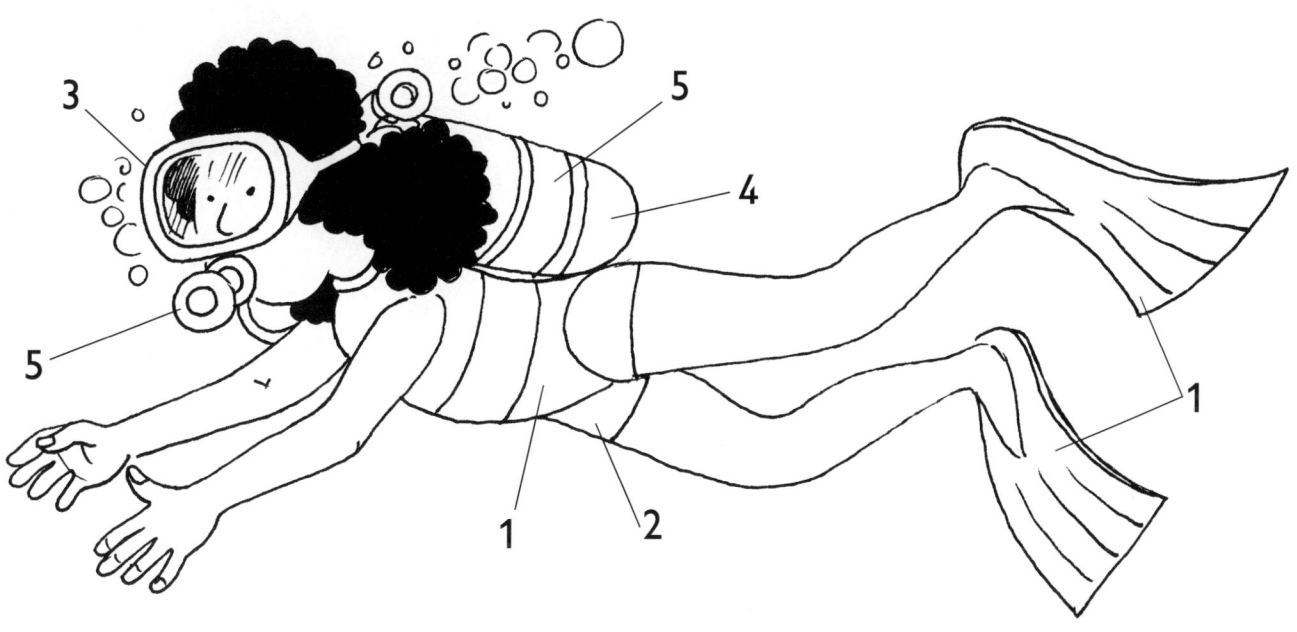

Look at page 20. Fill in the colour key for Wilma's swimming outfit.

1 _____

2 _____

3 _____

4 _____

5 _____

Colour the picture using the colour key.

Work
check

Here is a swimming certificate.

Fill in what the children have to do to pass the test.

SWIMMING CERTIFICATE

This is to certify that _____ can do all of these things:

1 ....

2 ....

3 ....

4 ....

5 ....

Signed ....

Fill in the name of one of the children who passed the test.

Write Mrs May's name on the bottom of the certificate.

Work
check

Main learning outcome: to read on sight high frequency words likely to occur in graded texts (W6)

Activity: Ask the children to read the words and colour in those they can read. The majority of these words are taken from Appendix List 2 and this sheet could be used for assessment purposes.

Main learning outcome: new words from reading linked to particular topics (W10)

Activity: The children fold the three panels to make a zigzag book in which they can write new words linked to a particular topic. They write the topic title and their names in the appropriate spaces. They could add small illustrations where appropriate.

Main learning outcome: to use simple poetry structures and to substitute own ideas, write new lines (T12)

Activity: The adult with the group reads the poem with the children and helps them hear the rhyme on lines two and three. The children underline the rhyming words. Then the children write two more verses to the poem using their own ideas.

Further activity: Children could write a further verse or illustrate their poem on the back of the sheet.

Name ______________________ Date ____________ AW Y2/T1

Colour in the words you can read.

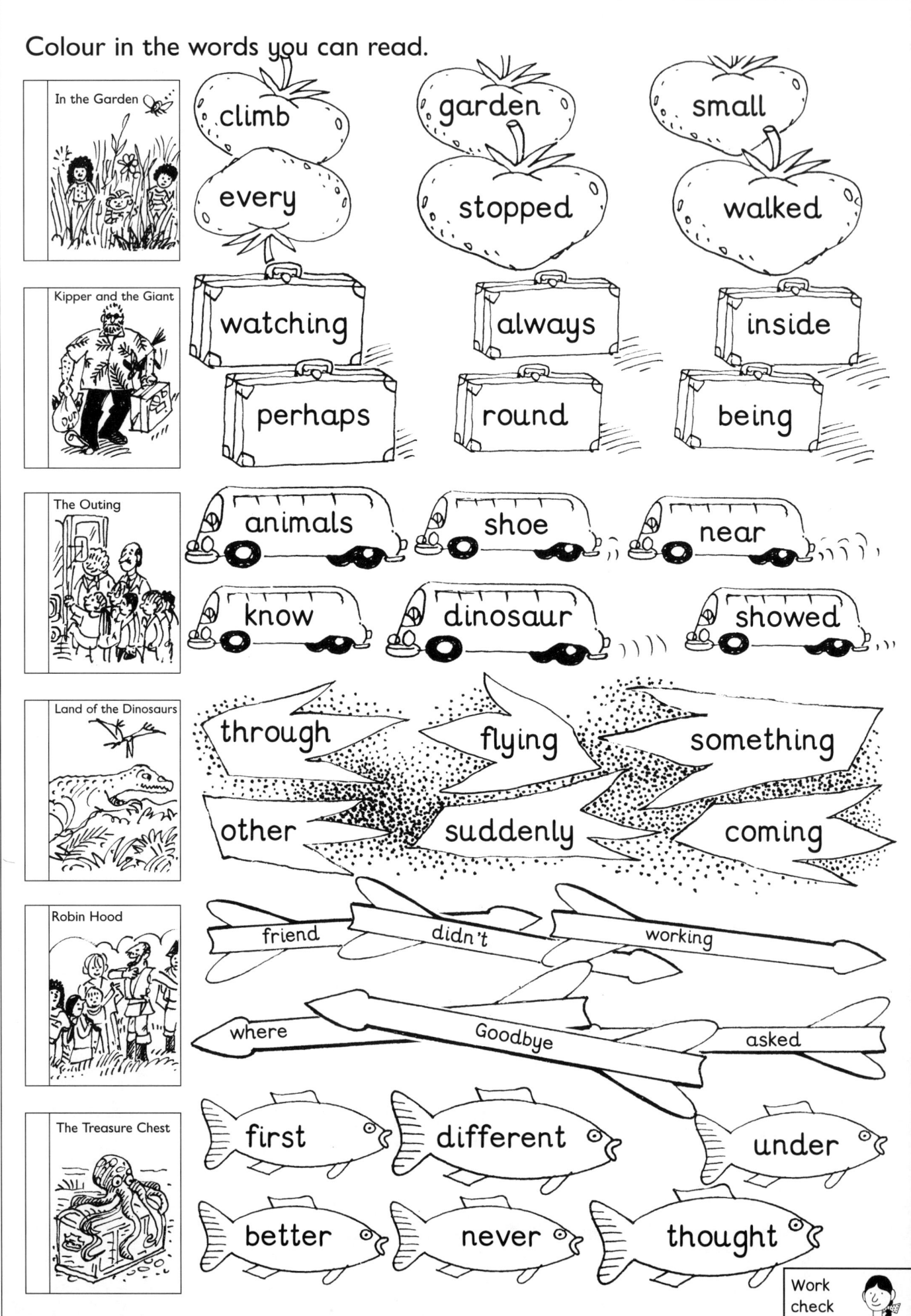

In the Garden

climb garden small
every stopped walked

Kipper and the Giant

watching always inside
perhaps round being

The Outing

animals shoe near
know dinosaur showed

Land of the Dinosaurs

through flying something
other suddenly coming

Robin Hood

friend didn't working
where Goodbye asked

The Treasure Chest

first different under
better never thought

Work check

© OUP 1999: this may be reproduced for class use solely within the purchaser's school or college

My collection of words
about

_____

fold

fold

'I like colours' by Pie Corbett (from Acorns Poetry - Colour Poems)

I like blue.
I like the sky
where birds fly high.

I like green.
I like frogs
as still as logs.

I like yellow.
I like the sun
when we have fun.

I like black.
I like the dark
when foxes bark.

Underline the rhyming words in each verse.
Write two more verses of your own on the lines below.

I like red.

I like _____

_____

_____

I like white.

I like _____

_____

Work
check

An excerpt from *The Treasure Chest* has been included and examples of its usage and the objectives that can be covered in Year 2 Term 1 are given below. These activities can be used with extracts from any of the books, but some extracts will obviously suit some objectives better than others.

Main learning outcomes: to secure identification of long vowel digraphs (W1); to revise and extend the reading of words containing different spellings of the long vowel phonemes (W2); to identify in writing and blend for reading the vowel phonemes *o, ar, oy, ow* (W3)

Activity: Ask the children to underline, highlight or put a ring round any of the vowel phonemes being targeted that week. Different colours could be used for different vowel phonemes.

Main learning outcome: to investigate and classify words with the same sounds but different spellings (W4)

Activity: Give the children the words to be investigated. The children would then find and list words in the text that sound the same but are spelled differently from the words given, e.g. ore/saw, know/no, blue/blew, sea/see, won/one, their/there.

Main learning outcome: to use word endings *s, ed* and *ing* to support their reading and spelling (W7)

Activity: Ask the children to underline in different colours the word ending given. The children could be given the verbs in the text that use all the endings and write them on the back of the sheet, e.g. look, like, open, point.

Main learning outcome: to use awareness of grammar to decipher new or unfamiliar words (S1)

Activity: Enlarge the extract or part of the extract, having deleted the words that are being investigated. Ask the children to fill in the missing words so that the text makes sense. The children can check their chosen words in the book.

Main learning outcome: to recognize and take account of commas and exclamation marks in reading aloud with appropriate expression (S3)

Activity: Ask the children to put different coloured rings around the commas and exclamation marks in the extract. The children then read the extract aloud, taking account of the punctuation.

Main learning outcomes: to reinforce and apply their word level skills through shared and guided reading (T1); to be aware of the difference between spoken and written language through comparing oral recounts with text (T3)

Activity: The children could read the excerpt in their guided reading time and then re-tell that part of the story in their own words.

Main learning outcome: to use language of time to structure a sequence of events (T11)

Activity: Choose and cut out suitable sentences from the text that could be preceded by words or phrases using the language of time, e.g. first, after a while, before, then, next, suddenly. Give the children the chosen sentences and a list of suitable link words or phrases. Ask the children to put the sentences in order preceded by a suitable link word or phrase.

Extract from *The Treasure Chest*

They saw an octopus.

Oh no! It was sitting on a chest.

They couldn't look inside the chest with an octopus sitting
  on the lid.

They blew bubbles at the octopus.

The octopus didn't like the bubbles so it swam away.

'Good!' thought the children.

'Now we can look inside.'

The children opened the chest and looked inside.

It was a treasure chest and it was full of gold.

Biff and Wilma pushed the chest over and all the gold fell out.

Nadim picked up a necklace and Biff picked up a gold cup.

Biff and Nadim were busy looking at the treasure.

They didn't see what Chip and Wilma saw.

A shark was coming.

Chip and Wilma couldn't tell Biff and Nadim.

They pulled them away and pointed at the shark.

The children were frightened.

They swam and swam but the shark swam after them.

Then the magic key began to glow.

The magic key took them out of the adventure.

'Wow! What an adventure!' said Biff.

'The treasure chest was like the one in our fish tank.'

The children ran to look in the fish tank.

'Look, there's the treasure,' said Chip.

'How did it get there?' asked Nadim.

'It's magic!' said Biff.

Work
check

Main learning outcome: the common spelling patterns for the vowel phonemes *air, or* and *er* (W2)

Activity: Ask the children to read the *air* words and then join the words to the right pictures. The children read the sentence with *or* words in and put a ring round all the sounds that say *or*. Then the children read the *er* words and write a sentence containing the *er* words given.

Further activity: Ask the children to write the various spellings of one of the vowel phonemes on the back of the sheet. The children find another word containing the vowel phonemes from their reading book or a dictionary and then write a sentence containing each word.

Main learning outcome: to be aware of the need for grammatical agreement in speech and writing, matching verbs to nouns and pronouns (S4)

Further outcome: to investigate and recognize other ways of presenting texts, e.g. speech bubbles (S7)

Activity: Ask the children to read the words the creatures are holding and choose the correct one to write on the line to complete each sentence. The children then choose 'am', 'is' or 'are' to put in the speech bubble to make what the creatures are saying correct.
N.B. This activity may be particularly difficult for children who have English as an additional language.

Further activity: Children could draw some space creatures on the back of the sheet and write relevant speech bubbles for them. Children could re-write the first three pairs of sentences substituting the correct pronoun for the subject of the sentence, e.g. He was playing.

Main learning outcome: to discuss and compare story themes (T3)

Activity: Ask the children to read the titles of the books in Stage 6 and Stage 7 from the back cover of the book. It would help to have a copy of each book to look at. Talk about the themes given on the worksheet and ask the children to choose two books which cover each theme. (Some books may cover more than one theme.) The children write the titles on the relevant pictures and answer the questions about themes.

Further activity: Children could write the reasons for their choice of favourite theme on the back of the sheet.

You can spell the sound that says **air** in different ways.

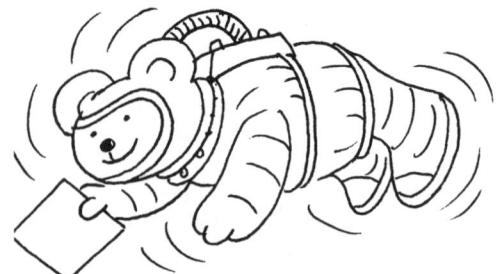

a b<u>ear</u> in the <u>air</u> with a squ<u>are</u>

Draw a line to join the words to the right pictures.

a hair in   a hare in   a pear in   a pair in
the air   the air   the air   the air

You can spell the sound that says **or** in different ways.
Put a ring round all the sounds that say **or** in this sentence.

Floppy caught more mice with his left paw on the floor of
the sports hall.

Write a sentence using these words which have the sound **er** in them.
Add more **er** words if you can.

birds   purple   were   over

Work
check

Look at the words the creatures are holding.

Choose the right word to complete each sentence and write it on the line.

Chip _____ playing.

Chip and Wilf _____ playing.

Floppy _____ up.

The dogs _____ up.

The rocket _____ off.

The rockets _____ off.

'I _____ falling,' said Floppy.

'We _____ falling,' said the children.

Make sure the creatures are saying the right thing.

Put **am**, **is** or **are** in the spaces.

Work check

STAGE 7: *Red Planet* **47**

Read the book titles on the back cover of the book.

The stories can be sorted into themes.

<u>Red Planet</u> has a **space** theme.

Choose two titles to write in the theme pictures.

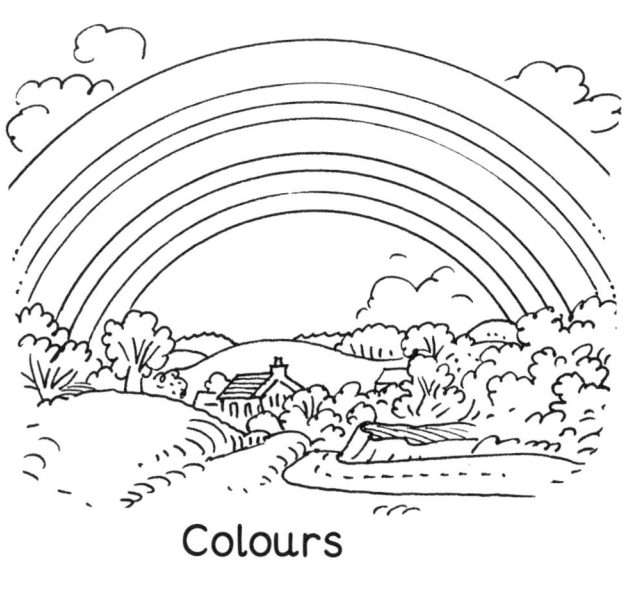

Colours

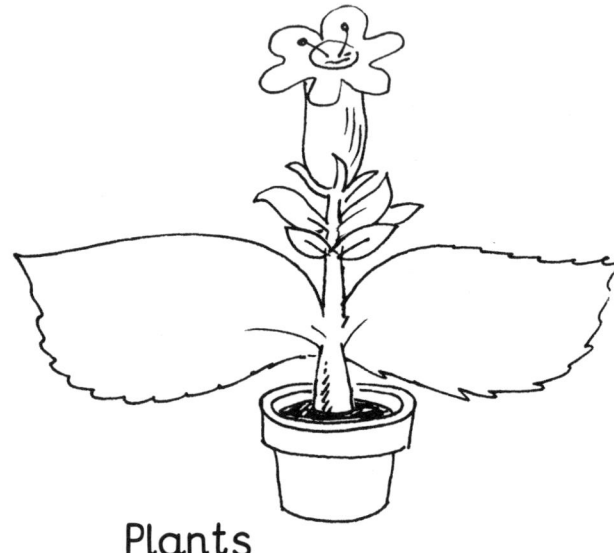

Plants

Transport

Past and present

Which is your favourite theme? _____

Which theme is the most exciting? _____

Which theme is the funniest? _____

Work check

Main learning outcome: to split familiar oral and written compound words into their component parts (W4)

Activity: Ask the children to read the first two sentences which give an example of a compound word. The children read the list of compound words and write the two separate parts on the lines. Then the children read the words which have fallen apart and write the correct compound words under each picture.

Further activity: Children could find further compound words which use one of the words in the river and write them on the back of the sheet, e.g. snowball, teaspoon, inside, outside, fireman.

Main learning outcome: to use verb tenses with increasing accuracy in speaking and writing, and to use past tense for narration (S5)

Activity: Ask the children to read the sentence that matches each picture and then change the sentence to say what happened as if they were telling a story. The children should write the new sentence on the line.

Further activity: Children could write three sentences on the back of the sheet about what they did yesterday. Each sentence could begin 'Yesterday I . . .' and should be written in the past tense.

Main learning outcome: to discuss story settings: to compare differences; to locate key words and phrases in text; to consider how different settings influence events and behaviour (T5)

Activity: Ask the children to look at the three pictures depicting the three settings of *Lost in the Jungle*. The children write what the setting is beneath each picture. They look in the book to find two things that could only be found in each setting and draw them in the relevant boxes. They then turn to the page numbers indicated and write a sentence about the monkey in each setting.

Further activity: Children could make lists of the characters that appear in each setting and write them on the back of the sheet.

It was Mum's birthday.

The word **birthday** can be split into two parts to make **birth** and **day**.

Split these words into two parts and write the parts on the lines.

greenhouse

nobody

waterfall

everything

goodbye

These words made with two parts fell apart in the waterfall.

Put them back together and write them under the correct pictures.

Work
check

Read what is happening in the pictures.
Then say what happened and write it down.

Biff is giving Mum a plant.

Biff gave Mum a plant.

Anneena is coming to play.

The magic is taking them to a jungle.

The children are seeing a monkey up a tree.

They are running through the jungle.

They are falling into a big net.

The lady is getting them down.

Work
check

The story <u>Lost in the Jungle</u> has three different settings.

Here are pictures of those settings.

Write what the settings are underneath the pictures.

Draw 2 things from each setting that can only be found in that setting.

....

A monkey appears in each setting. Write a sentence about the monkey in each setting. The page numbers will help you.

Page 1 At home ....

Page 9 In the jungle ....

Page 30 In the lost city ....

....

Work check

Main learning outcome: to discriminate syllables in multi-syllabic words using children's names and words from their reading. Extend to written forms and note syllable boundary in writing (W5)

Activity: Ask the children to read the first two sentences about syllables and name the characters holding the boxes. Children clap or tap with the syllables as they repeat the names and write the number of syllables in each character's name in the box they are holding.

Further activity: Children could write either the characters' names or their group's names on the back of the sheet and put strokes in each name to note where the syllable boundary occurs. Children could look through their reading book to find other words with a set number of syllables in and write them on the back of the sheet.

Main learning outcome: to identify speech marks in reading, understand their purpose, use the term correctly (S6)

Activity: Ask the children to turn to the pages listed to see if there are speech marks on that page. The children put a tick or cross as appropriate. The children turn to the next set of pages and draw a line to join the speaker to what they are saying on that page. The children then write what was said by the characters on the pages in question. Make sure they add the correct punctuation.

Further activity: On the back of the sheet children could draw one or two of the characters from the book with a speech bubble containing something that they said.

Main learning outcome: to identify and describe characters, expressing own views and using words and phrases from texts (T6)

Activity: Ask the children to write the names of the characters under their pictures, referring to the book for spelling if necessary. The children write who the characters from the past resemble in the present day situation. (Suggest that the children look at pages 16 and 17, and 5 and 21 if they cannot see the resemblance.) The children then answer the questions about their own views on the characters and choose a pair of matching characters to draw in the boxes.

Further activity: Children could choose one of the characters to describe on the back of the sheet and ask another child or the adult helper to guess who the character is from their description. They could draw the character if there is time.

The names Biff and Chip have 1 syllable each. Kipper has 2 syllables.

Write the number of syllables in each of the children's names.

Write the names of everyone in your group and write the number of syllables in each name.

_____ has _____ syllables.

_____ has _____ syllables.

_____ has _____ syllables.

_____ has _____ syllables.

_____ has _____ syllables.

_____ has _____ syllables.

Turn to page 32 of <u>The Broken Roof</u>.

Find and write some words with these numbers of syllables in.

2 words with 1 syllable are _____ and _____ .

2 words with 2 syllables are _____ and _____ .

1 word with 3 syllables is _____ .

Work check

Look in the book. Are there speech marks on these pages?
Put a tick for Yes (✓) and a cross for No (✗).

Page 1 (   )   Page 2 (   )   Page 3 (   )

Page 4 (   )   Page 5 (   )   Page 6 (   )

Page 7 (   )   Page 8 (   )   Page 9 (   )   Page 10 (   )

Look at these pages and join the speaker to what they are saying.

Page 2   'The field isn't a dump,'

Page 7   'The house looks very old,'

Page 11   'Oh no!'

Page 18   'We don't know,'

Page 20   'They have funny clothes,'

Page 23   'It won't be long now,'

Page 24   'We keep toys in here,'

Answer these questions. Don't forget the speech marks.

What did Anneena ask on page 3?

....

What did Biff ask on page 19?

....

What did Victoria ask on page 20?

....

What did Edward ask on page 29?

....

Work
check

Write the names of these characters.

....

These characters are from the past. Write who they are like in the present.

.... is like ....

.... is like ....

.... is like ....

.... is like ....

Turn to pages 16 and 17.

Which child looks the neatest? ....

Which child looks the funniest? ....

Whose clothes would you like to wear? ....

Which child would you like to play with? ....

Choose a matching pair of characters and draw their different clothes.

Work
check

Main learning outcome: to spell words with common prefixes, e.g. *un, dis,* to indicate the negative (W8)

Activity: Ask the children to look at the pictures and read the sentences which illustrate how a sentence can be made negative by putting *un* or *dis* in front of certain words. The children then read the second set of sentences and choose one of the prefixes to put in front of the underlined word to make the sentence say the opposite.

Further activity: Children could choose one of the underlined words and write two sentences of their own, one without the prefix and one with the prefix.

Main learning outcome: to investigate and recognize a range of other ways of presenting texts, e.g. speech bubbles, captions (S7)

Further outcome: to identify speech marks in reading, understand their purpose, use the term correctly (S6); to secure the use of simple sentences in own writing (S9)

Activity: Ask the children to tell the story in the comic strip by writing a simple caption and then filling in the speech bubbles appropriately.

Further activity: On the back of the sheet children could draw Kipper asleep with the key glowing from page 32 and write a simple caption for the picture.

Main learning outcome: to use story settings from reading, e.g. re-describe, use in own writing, write a different story in the same setting (T13)

Further outcome: through shared and guided writing to apply phonological, graphic knowledge and sight vocabulary to spell words accurately (T12)

Activity: Ask the children to write a short story about losing something in the park using the questions that the characters are asking as a guide to the story structure.

Further activity: Children could illustrate their story on the back of the sheet. Children could compare their story to the original and list the differences on the back of the sheet.

You can put **un** or **dis** in front of some words to make them say the opposite.

A key can **lock** a door.   A key can **unlock** a door.

Biff can **agree** with Chip.   Biff can **disagree** with Chip.

Put **un** or **dis** in front of the words which are underlined and write sentences which say the opposite.

Kipper was <u>lucky</u> to have lost the key.

Kipper was unlucky to have lost the key.

The key <u>appeared</u> in the grass.

_____

Kipper was <u>able</u> to find the key.

_____

The boys <u>obeyed</u> the man.

_____

Kipper was <u>happy</u> to lose the key.

_____

Mum <u>liked</u> paying for the key.

_____

Work
check

Tell the story in this comic strip. Fill in the speech bubbles.

Look at me, Mum!

Kipper has lost the key.

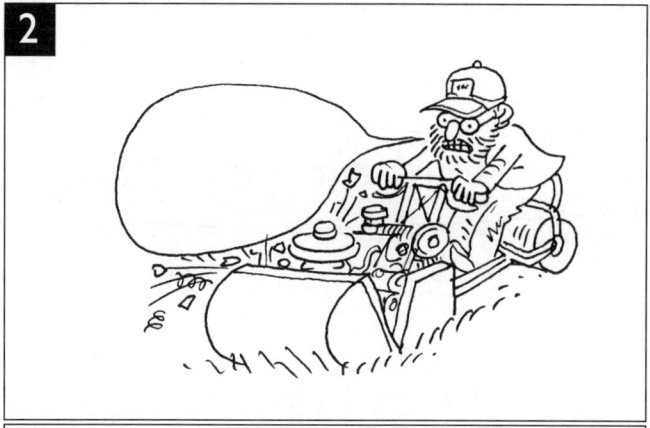

Work check

Write a short story about losing something in the park.

Here are some questions to help you.

 What did you lose?

 How did you lose it?

 What happened to it?

 Did you find it?

 How did you find it?

 Was it alright?

....

....

....

....

....

....

....

....

Work
check

Main learning outcome: the use of antonyms: collect, discuss differences of meaning and their spelling (W11)

Further outcome: to read on sight and spell words from Appendix List 1 (W6)

Activity: Ask the children to look at the pictures and read the descriptions below. The children read the lists of antonyms and join them with a line. The children then look at the pictures below and write the missing antonyms in the correct spaces, spelling the words from memory. Ask the children to read the sentence about the flowers and draw a common flower that they are familiar with and write its name.

Further activity: Children could choose two of the joined antonyms and write a sentence containing each one on the back of the sheet.

Main learning outcome: to use commas to separate items in a list (S8)

Activity: Ask the children to read the list of character names and point out the use of the comma. The children make a list of the names of the children in their group, putting a comma between each name. Then they make a list of the orchids illustrated, using commas. (The use of capital letters for the names of particular flowers could be mentioned.) Ask the children to write an appropriate name for the orchid in the oval.

Further activity: Children could turn to page 20 and make a list of the buildings shown on the map.

Main learning outcome: to use dictionaries to locate words by using initial letter (T16)

Further outcome: that dictionaries give definitions and explanations (T17)

Activity: Ask the children to find the words in a dictionary by using the initial letter and to write the definitions given. The children draw the missing illustrations.

Further activity: Children could write the words in alphabetical order on the back of the sheet. Children could choose other words from the story that they are not sure of, and write them and their definitions on the back of the sheet.

Name _____ Date _____

An **antonym** is a word which means the opposite to another.

 a **big** kite  a **little** kite  a **long** pole a **short** pole

Join the antonyms with a line.

near	strong
good	start
high	last
stop	far
happy	bad
weak	low
first	sad

Write the missing antonyms on the lines.

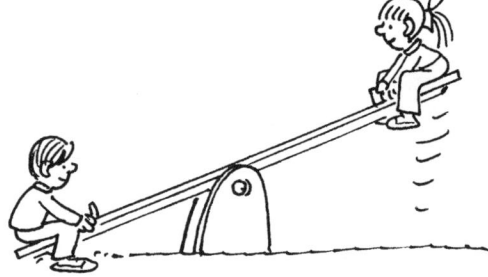

Biff went _____ Chip went _____

Floppy went _____ Kipper went _____

The flowers that the children found were **rare**.

The opposite of rare is **common**.

Draw a common flower and write its name.

This is a _____

Here is a list of the children in the <u>Oxford Reading Tree</u> books:

Kipper, Biff, Chip, Wilf, Wilma, Anneena, Nadim.

The items in the list have a comma to separate them.

Make a list of the children in your group. Don't forget the commas.

....

....

Gran found an orchid. Look at these pictures of orchids.

Bee Orchid

Fly Orchid

Frog Orchid

Lizard Orchid

Lady Orchid

Monkey Orchid

Make a list of these orchids.

....

....

....

Think of a name for this orchid.

....

Work check

STAGE 7: *The Motorway*   **63**

Find these words in a dictionary.

Write the definitions and draw the missing pictures.

shed ....

....

village ....

....

dragon ....

....

bulldozer ....

....

map ....

....

lake ....

....

Work
check

Main learning outcome: to use and practise the four basic handwriting joins (W14)

Further outcome: to practise handwriting in conjunction with the phonic and spelling patterns covered (W13)

Activity: Ask the children to copy the words in their best joined up handwriting.

Further activity: Children could write a sentence on the back of the sheet incorporating as many of the copied words as possible. Check that they still use the correct joins when they write a complete sentence.

Main learning outcome: to secure the use of simple sentences in own writing (S9)

Further outcome: to be aware of the need for grammatical agreement in writing, matching verbs to nouns/pronouns correctly (S4)

Activity: Ask the children to read the illustrated words in the box and then write a sentence to match each picture, using the words in the box to help them if necessary.

Further activity: Children could turn to pages 4 and 5 and write sentences on the back of the sheet to say what each character is holding in the picture.

Main learning outcome: to write character profiles, e.g. posters, using key words and phrases that describe or are spoken by characters in the text (T14)

Activity: Ask the children to fill in the WANTED poster for Rosie. Make sure that they find sentences about Rosie that do not contain the names already used.

Further activity: Children could draw Rosie with four big speech bubbles on the back of the sheet and write in the speech bubbles the four sentences that Rosie says on page 10 and 11.

Write these words in your
best handwriting or else . . .

are

not

with

bully

what

again

about

school

Write a sentence to match the picture.
You can use these words to help you.

Don't forget
the punctuation!

| holding | eating | crying |
| pointing | running | shaking |

STAGE 7: *The Bully*

Work
check

67

Name _____ Date _____

Fill in the missing words and sentences. Look in the book.

WANTED
FOR BULLYING

Rosie has called everyone names:

Chip is a

_____

Wilf is a

_____

Anneena is a

_____

Biff is a

_____

Wilma is a

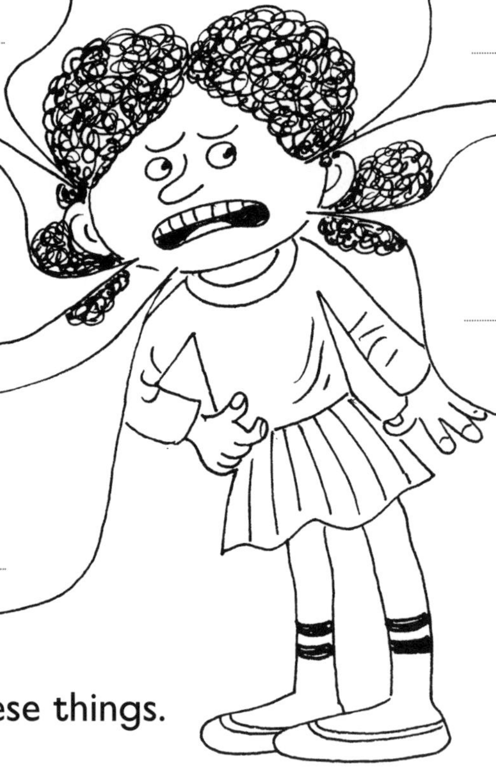

_____

Rosie has also done these things.

1. _____

2. _____

3. _____

4. _____

5. _____

Tell the teacher if you see her!

Work
check

Main learning outcome: to read and spell words containing the digraphs *wh, ph, ch* (W3)

Activity: Ask the children to read the words that surround the house and then circle them as they find them in the house. The words go both across and down. Ask the children to write the words on the appropriate list.

Further activity: Children could use a dictionary and write other words beginning with *ph* on the back of the sheet.

Main learning outcome: to read on sight high frequency words likely to occur in graded texts (W7)

Activity: Ask the children to read the words and colour in those they can read. Nearly all of these words are taken from Appendix List 2 and this sheet could be used for assessment purposes.

Main learning outcome: to use structures from poems as a basis for writing, by extending or substituting elements, inventing own lines (T15)

Activity: The adult with the group reads the poem with the children, explaining the more difficult words but concentrating on the days of the week. The children write their own poem about what they do on each day of the week. The weekday lines could say what they do in school on that day, e.g. singing on Monday, P.E. on Tuesday, etc.

The rhyme between Grundy, Monday and Sunday should also be mentioned, as well as the difficulty when writing a personal poem of a rhyming name.

Main learning outcome: that dictionaries give definitions and explanations; discuss what definitions are, explore some simple definitions in dictionaries (T17)

Further outcome: to use dictionaries to locate words by using initial letter (T16)

Activity: Ask the children to read about definitions and then to look at Floppy's dictionary and write the two definitions. Tell the children to use a dictionary to write the real definitions of the words and draw the pictures.

Main learning outcome: to use other alphabetically ordered texts, e.g. indexes, registers; to discuss how they are used (T18)

Activity: Ask the children to find a non-fiction book with an index in the back. Tell them to choose a word from the index that they find interesting and turn to the first page listed for that word. Ask them to find a sentence on the page that contains the word and to write it down. They should underline the chosen word. Then the children read the sentence with the children's names in and write the names in the register in alphabetical order.

Find the words containing **wh**, **ph** or **ch** in the house. They go across and down.

photograph

Christmas

P	S	T	C	O	R	C	H	I	D
H	Q	W	H	I	T	E	Y	U	C
O	E	L	E	P	H	A	N	T	H
T	V	B	W	N	F	D	E	L	R
O	X	A	H	I	J	O	W	K	I
G	S	U	A	M	W	L	H	W	S
R	P	G	T	B	K	P	E	C	T
A	V	T	R	A	O	H	N	Z	M
P	W	H	E	R	E	I	X	J	A
H	L	M	W	H	O	N	K	U	S

what

where

elephant

when

white

dolphin

who

orchid

Write the words in the right list.

<u>wh</u> words

<u>ph</u> words

<u>ch</u> words

....

....

....

....

....

....

....

....

....

....

....

....

Work check

Colour in the words you can read.

Red Planet

planet

place

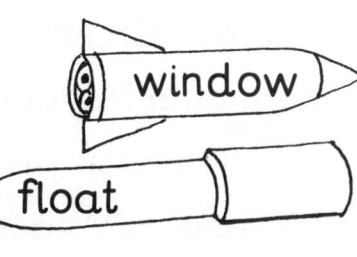
window

I'm

why

float

Lost in the Jungle

birthday

might

lady

think

years

today

The Broken Roof

clothes

use

does

woke

mother

until

The Lost Key

can't

started

same

still

asleep

sorry

The Motorway

higher	someone	right
between	before	shouted

The Bully

leave

tried

nobody

class

bigger

next

Work check

Read this poem about the life of a man called Solomon Grundy.

Solomon Grundy,
Born on a Monday,
Christened on Tuesday,
Married on Wednesday,
Took ill on Thursday,
Worse on Friday,
Died on Saturday,
Buried on Sunday.
This is the end
Of Soloman Grundy.

Write a poem about what you do on different days of the week.
Put your name on the first and the last line.

	Monday,
	Tuesday,
	Wednesday,
	Thursday,
	Friday,
	Saturday,
	Sunday.

This is the week

Of _____ .

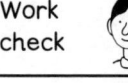

Work
check

A dictionary tells you what a word means. This is called a definition.
Floppy has his own dictionary. This is his definition for a tree.

 tree *something to sniff*

Write two more definitions for Floppy.

Floppy's Dictionary

bone _____

cat _____

Now look in a dictionary and write the real definitions.

Draw the real pictures.

tree _____

_____

bone _____

_____

cat _____

_____

Work
check

Find a non-fiction book with an index at the back.

Choose a word that you find interesting from the index.

Turn to the first page number for your chosen word.

Find a sentence with that word in and write it on the lines.

Underline your chosen word.

Kipper, Biff, Chip, Wilf, Nadim and Anneena are in a class with 4 other children Shazia, Lucy, Toby and Errol.

Write their names in alphabetical order in the register.

Name	Mon	Tues	Wed	Thurs	Fri

Work check

Main learning outcome: to use synonyms and other alternative words/phrases that express the same or similar meanings (W10)

Activity: Ask the children to read pages 26 and 27 of *The Kidnappers*. Explain that each gap on the sheet needs to be filled with a word that means the same as the word in the book. The children may choose a word from the box or think of one for themselves, then write it in the space provided. Tell the children to read the new story aloud to a partner to check that it makes sense.

Further activity: Ask the children to choose any four words from the box and find each one in a dictionary. They can write down the word and the definition on the back of the sheet.

Main learning outcome: to turn statements into questions using a range of *wh* question words and to use question marks (S6)

Activity: Read the first example with the children and show how the statement is turned into a question. Ask them if they can think of another question from this statement, e.g. Where did the magic take them to? Ask the children to make a question from each of the remaining sentences, then to make up one more question about the story.

Further activity: Ask the children to look at the question words on the aeroplane and to make up four more questions about the story using each of these words: Who? Where? When? What?

Main learning outcome: to understand the distinction between fact and fiction; to use terms 'fact' and 'fiction' appropriately (T13)

Activity: Look at the two examples and discuss why they are fact or fiction. Ask the children to look at each sentence in turn and decide what to write inside the van.

Further activity: Ask the children to make up two fictional sentences and write two facts about themselves. They can write all four sentences on the back of the sheet.

Read pages 26 and 27. Find a word in the box to fill each gap in these sentences. Keep the meaning of the story the same.

Bunbury set the _____ bears free.

Then they all _____ out of the window.

'Come on,' _____ Teddy. 'Follow me and

don't make a _____.'

The famous bears _____ into the honey van.

The nasty bears didn't _____ them because

they were too busy _____ the honey.

notice	licking	clambered	muttered
well-known	fuss	gulping	got	jumped
noise	tip-toed	important	whispered

What happened next? Write the rest of the story yourself.

_____

_____

_____

_____

Work
check

Change the sentences into questions, like this:

Sentence: The magic took them to an airport.

Where? Who? What? Where?

Question: What took them to an airport?

Sentence: They were going to Switzerland.

Question: _____

Sentence: Kipper went on an aeroplane to Switzerland.

Question: _____

Sentence: There was a bus at the airport.

Question: _____

Sentence: Kipper liked Switzerland.

Question: _____

Sentence: Kipper found a good place to   sit.

Question: _____

Sentence: A famous bear had come on to the stage.

Question: _____

Make up one more question about the story.

_____

Work
check

STAGE 8: *The Kidnappers*

Name _____ Date _____

Read these sentences. If the sentence is always true write **fact** on the van.
If it is only in a story, write **fiction** on the van.

Kipper's toys came to life. ——————————→

Aeroplanes can fly. ——————→

1 The magic took them to an airport. ———→

2 Airports can be very busy. ——→

3 Aeroplanes fly to Switzerland. ————→

4 Kipper had a magic adventure. →

5 Aeroplanes fly over lakes and mountains. →

6 You can catch a bus at an airport. →

7 Paddington is a famous bear. ————————→

Write one more sentence. Is it fact or fiction?

8 _____ →

Work
check

Main learning outcome: to reinforce work on discriminating syllables in reading and spelling from previous term (W2)

Activity: Remind the children that a syllable is a 'beat' in a word. Clap the syllables of children's names to reinforce their understanding. Look at the examples with the children and ask them to write the next words with one letter on each dash, and write the number of syllables in the box. Then they need to find words to fit the right number of letters and syllables from the words in the longship.

Further activity: Ask the children to look through the book and find as many words as possible with five letters. They can make a list then write the number of syllables beside each word, e.g. about 2, bears 1.

Main learning outcome: to use standard forms of verbs in writing and to use the past tense consistently for narration (S3)

Activity: Read the first sentence with the children and try the alternative words from the brackets. Which one sounds best for telling a story? Ask them to continue with the other sentences, choosing the right word from those in the brackets. Then ask them to write what they remember about the story after the children had been found. Encourage them to write without referring back to the book.

Further activity: Children can continue the story on the back of the sheet or write what Biff and Wilf said to Mr Johnson to explain where they got the shield.

Main learning outcome: to invent language puzzles derived from reading (T11)

Activity: Show the children how to find the right page, line and word by using the list of clues. Help them to find the right place to write the first word. Show them that there is a hidden word in the bold box, reading downwards, if all the clues are correctly solved. For the second crossword, point out that the words have been written in, but that they need to look for the page, line and word numbers to write the clues.

Further activity: Use squared paper to draw a large square containing four squares across and four squares down. Ask the children to find four 4-letter words in the story and write them inside the puzzle square. Then they can use the book to write a clue for each word in the same way. Finally, tell them to draw a new blank square and write the clues neatly. Each child can ask a friend to solve the puzzle, or the puzzles could be collected into a puzzle book.

Name ______________________ Date ______________ I W Y2/T3

Biff is a word with 1 syllable. → Biff ___ ___ ___ ___ → [1] syllable

Adventure has 3 syllables.

Adventure → ___ ___ / ___ ___ ___ / ___ ___ ___ ___ → [3] syllables

Split these words into syllables.

Viking → ___ ___ / ___ ___ ___ ___ → [ ] syllables

nobody → ___ ___ / ___ ___ ___ / ___ → [ ] syllables

suddenly → ___ ___ ___ / ___ ___ ___ / ___ ___ → [ ] syllables

longship → ___ ___ ___ ___ / ___ ___ ___ ___ → [ ] syllables

villagers → ___ ___ ___ / ___ ___ ___ / ___ ___ ___ → [ ] syllables

Choose a word from the ship to match these syllables.

___ ___ ___ ___ → [ ] syllable

___ ___ ___ ___ / ___ ___ ___ ___ → [ ] syllables

___ ___ ___ ___ / ___ ___ / ___ ___ ___ → [ ] syllables

___ ___ / ___ ___ ___ / ___ ___ ___ / ___ ___ ___ → [ ] syllables

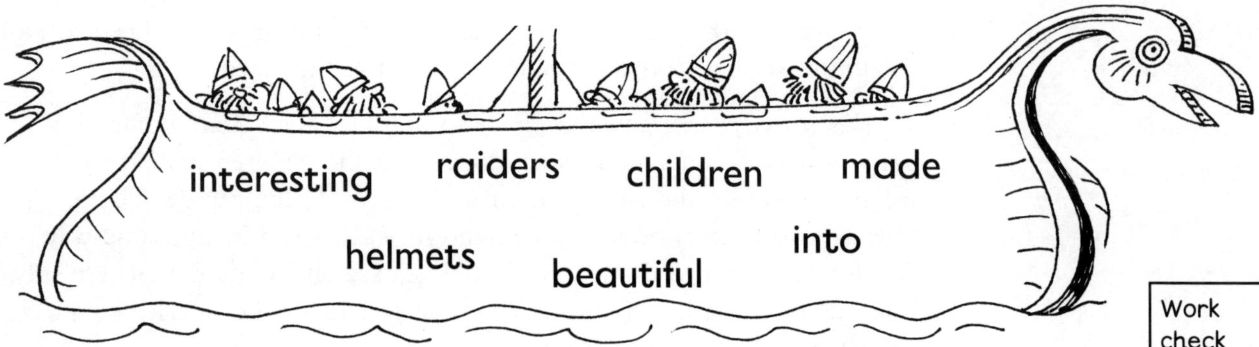
interesting
raiders
children
made
helmets
beautiful
into

Work check

Choose the right word to fill the gaps.

The children _____ home from school.

(come   came   coming)

They _____ at the magic key.

(look   looked   looking)

The magic key _____ working after all.

(were   was   is)

The Vikings _____ the longship across the sea.

(row, rowed, rowing)

One of the Vikings _____ to get the sail.

(goes, went, going)

What happened next? Go on with the story.

_____

_____

_____

_____

_____

_____

_____

Work
check

Use the clues to find each word in the puzzle.

You will find a hidden word written in the box.

Clues

1: page 15 line 3 word 3

2: page 16 line 1 word 5

3: page 17 line 5 word 5

4: page 18 line 3 word 3

5: page 19 line 4 word 4

6: page 20 line 4 word 2

The hidden word is _____ .

Write clues for this crossword. (Use pages 25–30.)

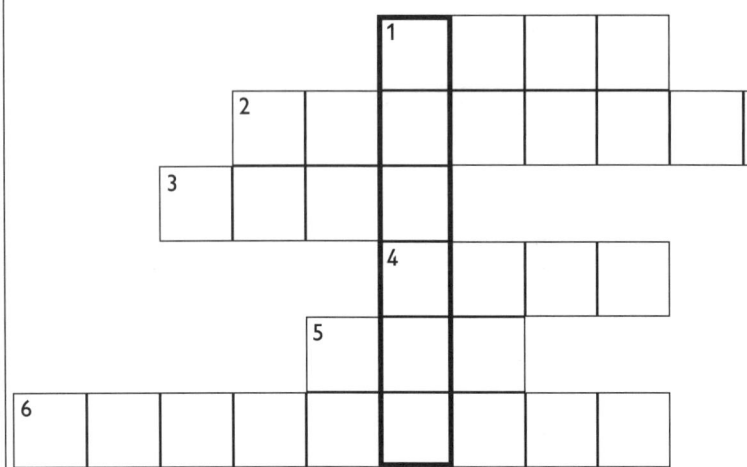

¹r	a	n			
²a	t	t	a	c	k
³i	d	e	a		
⁴s a i l e d					
⁵t	h	e	y		
⁶p	a	r	t	y	

Clues

1: page ____ line ____ word ____

2: page ____ line ____ word ____

3: page ____ line ____ word ____

4: page ____ line ____ word ____

5: page ____ line ____ word ____

6: page ____ line ____ word ____

The hidden word is _____ .

Work check

Main learning outcome: to investigate words which have the same spelling patterns but different sounds (W6)

Activity: Look at the first set of three words with the children and ask them to read the words aloud. Which word does not rhyme with the other two? That word is written in the rectangle. Ask them to do the same for each set of words. When the children have completed the list, ask them to look at words in the rectangles in turn and think of a word that rhymes with each one. They write the word they have thought of in the oval. This time the spelling pattern may be different, e.g. to rhyme with 'to' children could write 'do' or 'blue' or 'flew'.

Further activity: Ask the children to list all the words they can make ending in *ow*. When they have at least ten words ask them to sort out the lists so that they have words that rhyme with 'low' and words that rhyme with 'cow'. Do any words belong in both lists, e.g. 'bow'? (Words include: bow, blow, brow, cow, crow, flow, glow, grow, how, low, mow, now, prow, row, sow, slow, stow, tow, vow.)

Main learning outcome: to write in clear sentences using capital letters and full stops accurately (S5)

Activity: Ask the children to tell you what they remember about Fred. Read the first sentence together and explain that each sentence should begin beside the next number on a new line. Encourage children to compose their own sentences using the words listed for help with ideas. Remind them that the sentences need to be about Fred, not just re-telling the story.

Further activity: Tell the children to exchange sentences with a partner. They should read their partner's sentences and check that they all make sense. Remind them to check that their partner has used a capital letter at the beginning of each sentence and a full stop at the end.

Main learning outcome: to read and respond imaginatively to humorous stories (T6)

Further outcome: through shared and guided reading to apply phonological, graphic knowledge and sight vocabulary to spell words accurately (T9)

Activity: Ask the children to remind each other about everything that happened when the rainbow machine went wrong. Which rainbow did they think was the funniest? Discuss other weather-making machines, such as a snow machine. How might they go wrong? Ask the children to write their stories independently, continuing on to the back of the sheet if they want to. Ask them to read the stories aloud during the final part of the lesson.

Further activity: Remind the children to read through their stories to check their spelling when they have finished. Ask them to underline any spelling they think may not be correct then to look in word banks or dictionaries to check the words.

Some words have the same spelling pattern but do not rhyme. Find the word that does not rhyme with the other two. Write it in the rectangle.

Odd one out

1 no   go   to   [to] rhymes with ( )

2 good food hood   [ ] ⟶ ( )

3 one stone done   [ ] ⟶ ( )

4 said afraid paid   [ ] ⟶ ( )

5 call tall shall   [ ] ⟶ ( )

6 push rush bush   [ ] ⟶ ( )

7 work fork cork   [ ] ⟶ ( )

8 lorry sorry worry   [ ] ⟶ ( )

9 what flat that   [ ] ⟶ ( )

Now think of a word to rhyme with each word in the rectangle.
Write it in the oval.

[to] rhymes with (do)

Write five more sentences about Fred.

Remember a capital letter at the beginning of each sentence and a full stop at the end.

1 Fred was one of the rainbow makers.

2 _____

_____

3 _____

_____

4 _____

5 _____

6 _____

_____

Remember your sentences must be about Fred.

These words will help you:

| new | learning | stuck | field |

| asked | drove | computer |

Work check

The story of <u>The Rainbow Machine</u> is funny when the machine goes wrong.

Think of a machine for other kinds of weather.

Write your ideas in the box before you begin.

My machine ....

Who is in charge of the machine? ....

What goes wrong? ....

The .... Machine

Work check

Main learning outcome: to spell words with the suffix *ly* (W7)

Activity: Children are asked to add *ly* to a list of words. These words are missing from the part of the story re-told below. Ask the children to find one of their *ly* words to fit in each gap. Although some words fit in more than one place, it is possible to use a different word each time.

Further activity: Ask the children to choose any four of the *ly* words from the list. On the back of the sheet ask them to write a sentence using each of the four words they have chosen.

Main learning outcome: the need for grammatical agreement, matching verbs to nouns and pronouns; using simple gender forms (his/her) correctly (S2)

Activity: This is what the boy tells Biff and Kipper on pages 18 and 19. All the missing words are printed on the carpet. Encourage the children to try to fill the gaps without reference to the book. They will need to read and re-read the sentences to check that it all makes sense. They may need help to notice that it is written in the present tense and should not change to the past part way through.

Further activity: Ask the children to check their sheet by referring to pages 18 and 19 of the story. On the back of the sheet they can copy out page 20, missing out the words that are written on the carpet and drawing lines in the gaps with a ruler. They can ask their partner to fill in the gaps.

Main learning outcome: to use phonological, contextual, grammatical and graphic knowledge to work out, predict and check the meanings of unfamiliar words and to make sense of what they read (T2)

Activity: Children usually find it difficult to explain what words mean. Talk about junk and what it is. What else could you write instead of 'second-hand things'? Ask the children to read the other words and write down what they would say to explain what the words mean. They should attempt their own spellings. The second part of the sheet asks children to link words that mean the same or nearly the same.

Further activity: Provide dictionaries and ask the children to find four of the words and write the definitions on the back of the sheet. The children's ideas and the dictionary definitions can be discussed during the final part of the lesson.

Name _____ Date _____

Add **ly** to these words.

sudden ⟶	wise ⟶ ....
sad ⟶	safe ⟶ ....
quick ⟶	slow ⟶ ....
quiet ⟶	brave ⟶ ....
immediate ⟶	bad ⟶ ....
silent ⟶	kind ⟶ ....

Write an **ly** word in each gap in the story.

.... the magic key began to glow.

The carpet flew .... over deserts and mountains.

It .... stopped by a window.

Biff and Chip climbed .... into the room.

'I am the real king of this land,' said the boy ....

'I promised to rule the country .... and well.

My uncle rules ....'

'We must set you free .... ,' said Biff.

'The carpet will take us .... to your mother.'

The soldiers fought ....

Work check

Find the missing words on the magic carpet. Write them in the gaps.

_____ uncle _____ a bad man. _____ cruel and greedy. _____ makes the people pay money even if _____ poor. If _____ can't pay, _____ puts _____ in prison. Nobody _____ happy. Every day the people ask _____ mother and _____ army to attack the city. _____ will not give the order to attack because _____ afraid _____ uncle will harm _____ .

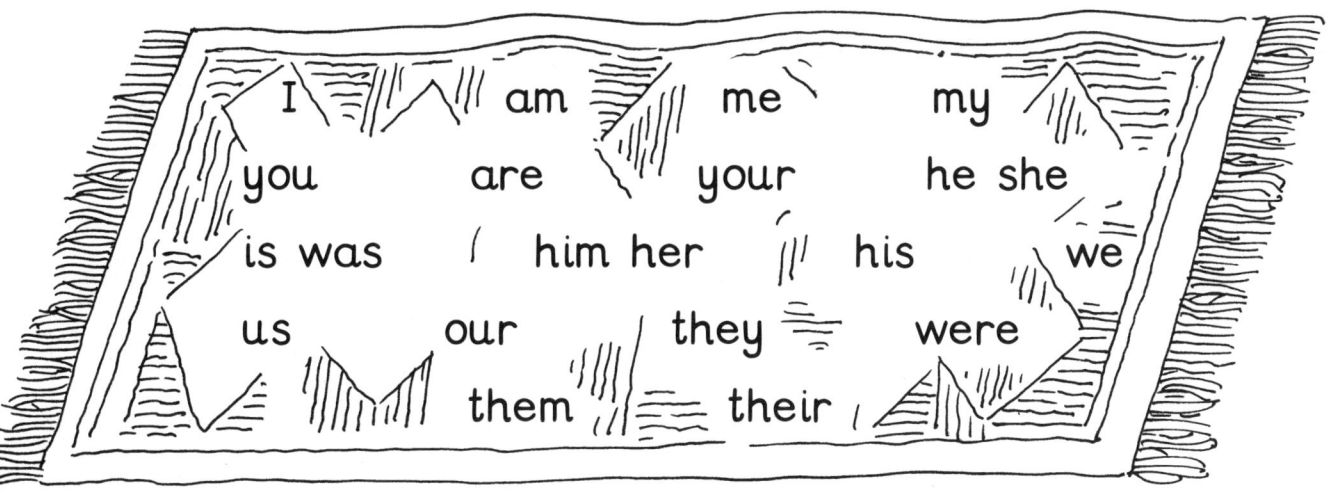

I   am   me   my
you   are   your   he she
is was   him her   his   we
us   our   they   were
them   their

Work check

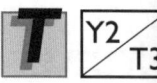

Use the story and the pictures to help you to explain what these words mean.

(page 2)   Junk means _____

(page 10)   A tower is _____

(page 15)   Wicked means _____

(page 16)   To rule the country means _____
_____

(page 16)   A jealous person is someone who _____
_____

(page 19)   A hostage is _____

(page 22)   Sped means _____

Join words that mean nearly the same thing.

set free   wicked

cruel   unhappily

sadly   escape

battle   prison

jail   fight

Work
check

Main learning outcome: to discriminate, read and spell the phonemes *ear* (hear) and *ea* (head) (W3)

Further outcomes: to secure phonemic spellings from previous five terms (W1)

Activity: Ask children to look for words in the wordsearch puzzle that have *ea* in them. If it sounds like 'ear' the word is written on Floppy's ear. If it sounds like 'head', it is written on Floppy's head. Finally, the children can count the number of words for each phoneme.

Further activity: Remind the children that words spelt *ea* can also sound like *ee*. Ask them to use the back of the sheet to write words that rhyme with 'meat'.

Main learning outcome: to compare a variety of questions from texts (S7)

Activity: Look at page 3 with the children and find the question 'What are they?' Ask the children why Kipper is asking this question. Tell the children to look for more questions in the book, starting with one on page 7. Ask them to write it in the speech bubble. Then ask them to find two more questions in the story and write them in the bubbles. Finally, ask the children to look at page 25 and suggest what the lady in charge might say if she had seen Gran among the waxworks. Tell them to write the question inside the speech bubble. Discuss their different questions.

Further activity: Write three more questions that Mum or Dad might have asked when they saw the car come back on the break-down lorry.

Main learning outcome: to write sustained stories using their knowledge of story elements; narrative, settings, and the language of story (T10)

Further outcome: to apply phonological, graphic and sight vocabulary to spell words accurately (T9)

Activity: Let each child decide whether he or she is going to write an account of a day in London or a story. Encourage them to discuss with a partner the different ways they might begin the story and add some suggestions in the box. Ask them to look in the book for more settings in London and add them to the list with any other places they might want to include. Then they need to note the main event of the story, adding more than one idea to the box if they can. Finally, ask the children to think of a way for the story to end.

Further activity: Use the story format sheet on page 128. Ask the children to write the title, author and to begin to write the story using the planning sheet.

Circle words with **ea** phonemes.

If the phoneme sounds like ea in **'ear'**, write it on Floppy's ear.

If it sounds like ea in **'head'** write it on Floppy's head.

h	e	a	d	k	e	a	r
p	a	c	l	e	a	r	l
w	e	a	t	h	e	r	e
d	e	a	f	d	e	a	r
t	h	r	e	a	d	r	t
i	n	s	t	e	a	d	h
s	p	r	e	a	d	a	e
h	e	a	r	f	e	a	r
p	g	e	a	r	n	t	a

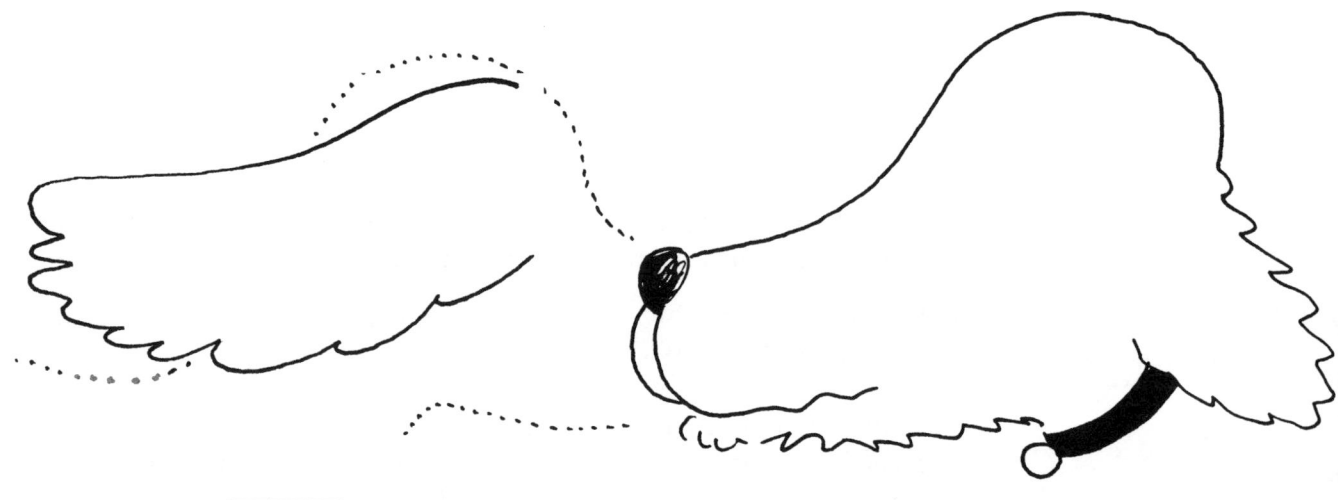

I found  words that rhyme with 'ear'.

I found  words that rhyme with 'head'.

Work check

What are they?

Find three more questions in the story.

Write them in the speech bubbles.

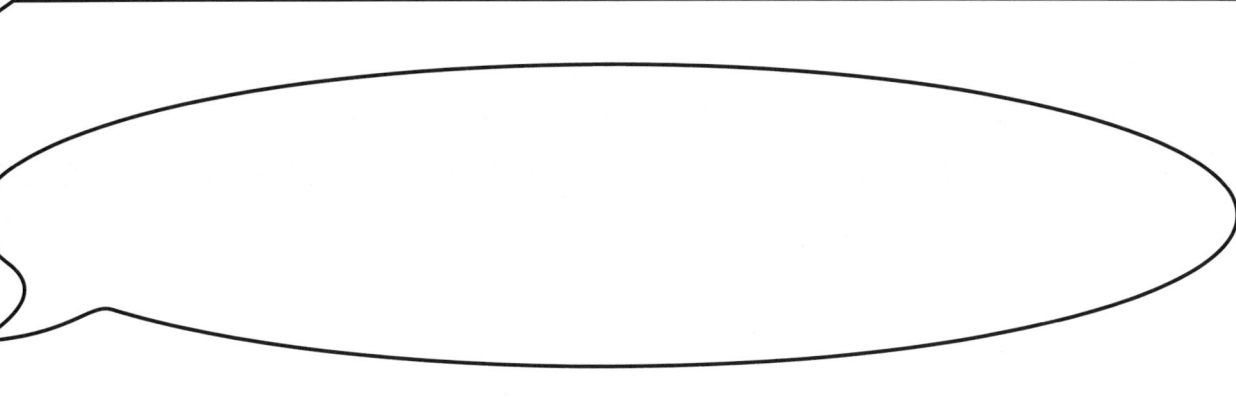

Look at page 25. Write a question that the lady at the waxworks might have asked Gran.

Work check

Plan a story called <u>A day in London</u>.

It can be true (fact) or imaginary (fiction).

Starting the story:

| Last Saturday . . . | In the Easter holidays . . . |
| For a special treat . . . | We had never been to London . . . |

Or _____

Choose a setting or settings:

| The Science Museum | The Natural History Museum |
| The National Gallery | Millennium Dome |

Or _____

The adventure or best part of the trip:

Lost in a toy shop – announcement – loud speakers

Ride on an open-topped bus and saw . . .

Got on the wrong tube train and ended up at . . .

Or _____

_____

_____

At the end :

_____

Work check

Main learning outcome: to secure spelling of all the high frequency words in Appendix List 1 (W4)

Activity: Ask children to write the missing words in the sentences from the story. The boxes are provided to help the children think of the correct word. In some words a letter is written in to provide an extra clue. Then ask the children to fill in the next set of boxes with names of colours.

Further activity: Ask the children to make puzzles in the same way for number words (not in order!). They will need to draw boxes to show letters with ascenders and descenders and can put one letter in each for a clue if they want to. These puzzles can then be passed to a friend for completion or used during the plenary session to reinforce number word spellings.

Main learning outcome: to use commas in lists (S4)

Activity: Read the first sentence with the children, drawing their attention to the commas and to the fact that there is no comma before 'and'. Ask them to use the story to complete the other sentences with lists, using commas correctly.

Further activity: Ask the children to look at pages 30 and 31 and make a list of all the things the illustrator has drawn in the throne room, leaving out the characters. Finish this sentence: 'Alex Brychta has drawn curtains, . . .'

Main learning outcome: to compare books by the same author: settings, characters, themes (T4)

Further outcome: to compare books by the same author; to evaluate and form preferences, giving reasons (T4)

Activity: Help the children to use the chart to list the settings, characters and themes in each of the three stories at Stage 8. As children need to summarize the setting and the theme, it will be helpful if an adult is available to help. Some parts have been filled in to show the children what is expected.

Further activity: On the back of the sheet ask the children to write 'The story I like best is _____ because _____.' Encourage them to think of three reasons why that book is their favourite.

Fill in the gaps in this story. Spell the words yourself.

The words must fit the boxes. Sometimes there is a letter clue to help you.

The magic took them ☐☐☐ in time to a street on

a foggy ☐☐ .

They followed Vicky ☐☐☐ winding streets. At

☐☐ t they ☐☐☐ to a blacksmith's. The

blacksmith was ☐☐☐☐☐☐ at a horse's hoof.

☐☐ horse needed a ☐ e ☐ shoe.

'I'll give ☐☐ a penny ☐☐ pump the bellows,'

☐☐☐ the ☐☐☐ s m i t ☐ .

Use the clues to write seven colours.

☐☐☐   ☐☐☐   ☐☐ y

☐☐☐ w   ☐☐ l ☐

☐☐☐ n   ☐☐☐ n

The adult characters in <u>Victorian Adventure</u> are Gran, a blacksmith, Queen Victoria, some grown-ups, a policeman and an important man.

Notice that you need a comma after each person or thing in the list but not before 'and'.

Finish these sentences with lists.

The children in <u>Victorian Adventure</u> are Biff,

....

....

The games they played in the Palace were hide and seek,

....

....

Victorian things you can see in this story are a gas lamp,

....

....

Work
check

This table compares three stories by Roderick Hunt.
Finish the entries for the books.

Title	Setting	Characters	Theme
The Kidnappers	A teddy bears' picnic in Switzerland	Kipper . . .	Famous bears are kidnapped.
The Rainbow Machine	A showery day in the countryside	Nadim . . .	Making . . .
Victorian Adventure			

Work check

Main learning outcome: to spell words with common suffixes, e.g. *ful* (W7)

Further outcome: to spell words with common suffixes *ly* (W7)

Activity: Ask the children to find the missing word by checking page 10 of the story. Show them that 'careful' is made from 'care' + 'ful'. Ask them to make more words in the same way. Point out that there is only one 'l' in 'ful'. Then explain that one word from the list will fill each of the gaps in the sentences. Finally, there are two words to find in a dictionary and space to write the meanings.

Further activity: Ask the children to add *ly* to each word in the list. 'Careful' becomes 'carefully', etc. Then ask them to make up sentences using one of the words in each, e.g. 'They looked carefully in all the rock pools.'

Main learning outcome: to turn statements into questions, learning a range of *wh* words to open questions (S6)

Activity: Explain that this is the reporter's notebook and the reporter asked Chip some questions about the adventure. Chip's answers are on the pad. The children need to write the questions that would get these answers. Question words are in the thought bubbles.

Further activity: Reporters call their reports 'stories'. They need to know the names of all the people, what they did and why they did it. Make up three more questions starting 'Who...?' , 'What...?' and 'Why...?'

Main learning outcome: to write their own riddles and language puzzles (T11)

Further outcome: to apply phonological, graphic knowledge and sight vocabulary to spell words correctly (T9)

Activity: Show the children how to complete the puzzles by solving the first two clues with them. Ask them to finish the puzzle and do the next one on their own. Show them that for the last puzzle the word has been completed, but they need to make up the clues. Words in the boat could be used in their clues, e.g. 'Take the last letter from crab....'

Further activity: Ask the children to take a three- or four-letter word from the story and make up the clues themselves. Words could be 'sea', 'gull', 'pool'. Suggest the children give their puzzle to a friend to solve.

Find the missing word on page 10.

Oil is hard to get off, so be _____ , everyone.

care + ful ———→ careful

Change these words.

harm + ful ———→ _____

rest + ful ———→ _____

cheer + ful ———→ _____

wonder + ful ———→ _____

colour + ful ———→ _____

Choose a word from your list to fill the gaps in these sentences.

_____ means you look happy.

_____ means brightly coloured.

_____ means quiet and gentle.

Look for these words in a dictionary.

Harmful means _____

Wonderful means _____

Work check

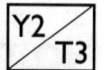
The reporter has written down Chip's answers.
Write the questions the reporter asked.

Who? What? Which? Where?

How many? Why?

Toxic waste story

Question: Which island were you on?

Chip: We were on Green Island.

Question: _____

Chip: We were exploring and looking at sea birds.

Question: _____

Chip: The drums were hidden in a small cave.

Question: _____

Chip: Four people got out of the boat.

Question: _____

Chip: Mrs Honey told us what to do.

Question: _____

Chip: We took their boat so that they couldn't get off the island.

Work check

Use the clues to spell words from the story.

Take the second letter from spill,
the first from oar,
the last from oil.
Then take the second vowel in toxic,
the beginning from crab,
and the end from cave.
What am I?

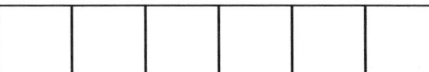

Take the only letter in I,
The last from dangerous
And the end of tunnel.
Take the middle from small
And the end of green.
Finish with the beginning of drum.
What am I?

Write the clues for this word.

b	o	a	t

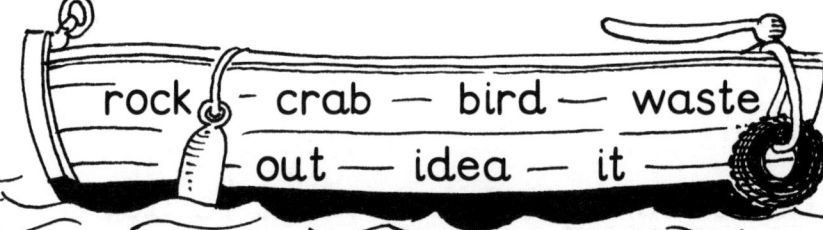

rock — crab — bird — waste
out — idea — it

You could use the words on the boat in your clues.

....

....

....

What am I?

Work
check

Main learning outcome: to use synonyms and other alternative words/phrases that express same or similar meanings (W10)

Activity: Read Kipper's question and the monster's answer with the children. Ask them to write the answer to each of the following questions in the same way, in the speech bubbles. If they find it too difficult to explain the meanings in their own words, the children can use a dictionary.

Further activity: If a dictionary was not used for the main activity, ask the children to check the meanings they have written down by looking up each word in a dictionary. Then ask them to use a dictionary to write down the meanings for 'computer', 'spacecraft' and 'desert'.

Main learning outcome: to use standard forms of verbs in writing and to use the past tense consistently for narration (S3)

Activity: Ask the children to read the story, using words from the castle to fill in the gaps. Remind them to read the whole page to themselves before they finish to check that the story sounds right.

Further activity: Ask the children to write the end of the story, explaining why Chip was not afraid of the nasty-looking robot.

Main learning outcome: to write tongue twisters (T11)

Further outcome: to write alliterative sentences (T11)

Activity: Discuss tongue twisters and read the examples given. Ask the children to use some of the words listed to make up a robot tongue twister. Then ask them to read the instructions and complete the rest of the sheet. The children could read out their tongue twisters in the plenary session.

Further activity: Ask the children to make up a sentence about Chip using as many *ch* words as possible, e.g. 'Chip chooses cherries and cheese.' Then tell them to choose another character's name to make a sentence with words beginning with the same sound, or to use their own name.

What's a maze?

A maze is a kind of puzzle. You have to find the right path to get through it.

Explain what these words mean.

| What is a robot? | A robot is |

| What is a castle? | A castle is |

| What is a mirror? | A mirror is |

| What is a keyhole? | A keyhole is |

Work check

Choose the right words to tell the story.

Storm Castle

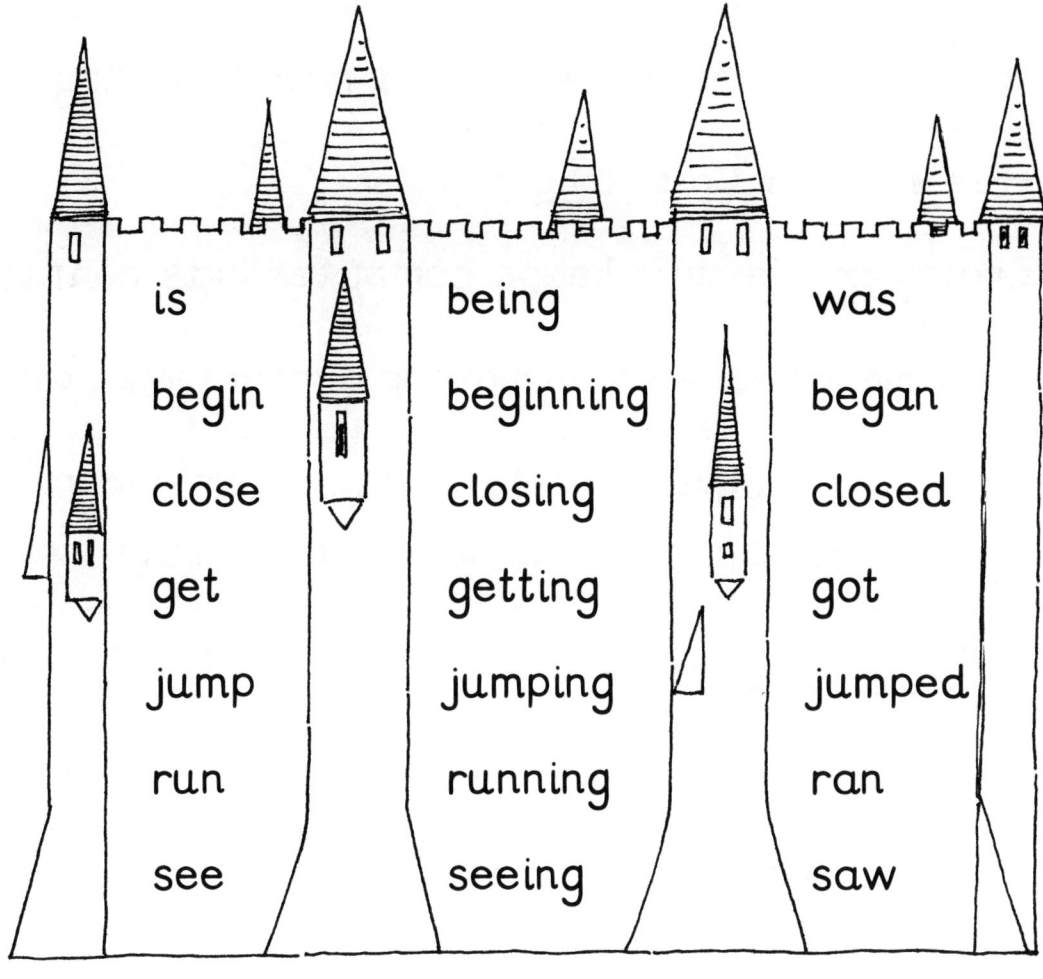

is	being	was
begin	beginning	began
close	closing	closed
get	getting	got
jump	jumping	jumped
run	running	ran
see	seeing	saw

Storm Castle _____ in front of them. The children

_____ a bridge. Suddenly, the bridge _____ to

open in the middle. Biff and Kipper _____ as fast as

they could. Then they _____ across. The gate of the

castle was _____ . It was _____ lower and

lower. They _____ under the gate just in time.

Work
check

Tongue twisters are difficult to say because the words sound alike.

'Round and round the rugged rock the ragged rascal ran.'

Here is a Storm Castle tongue twister.

Crafty castle quiz keeps computer kids confused.

Use some of these words to make up a robot tongue twister.

rumbling	rusty	rush	remember	really
round	roll	rubbish	ruin	rain	risk	real

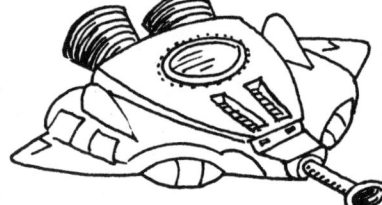

....

....

Now try 'magic mirror' and 'mighty monster' tongue twisters using some of these words.

make	many	monsters	mighty	mischief	mirror
magnify	magnificent	mad	mainly	might	mistake
monstrous	moody	model	magic	muddle

....

....

....

....

Work check

Main learning outcome: to investigate words with the same spelling patterns but different sounds (W6)

Activity: This sheet follows the same pattern as the word work for *The Rainbow Machine*. Children may know what to do without any help. Explain that the three words on each line have the same spelling patterns, but one sounds different. The 'odd one out' is to be written in the rectangle. After all ten 'odd words out' have been identified the children need to think of words that rhyme with them. They should then write them inside the ovals. The words in the ovals may or may not have the same spelling pattern, e.g. 'bear' rhymes with 'pear', but also with 'care' and 'fair'. The different patterns will encourage children to revise patterns learned in previous terms.

Further activity: Ask the children to look at each set of three words again. Can they think of one more word for each spelling pattern, but not one they have written in the oval? They can write the new word on the back of the sheet.

Main learning outcome: to write in clear sentences using capital letters and full stops accurately (S5)

Activity: Read the first sentence with the children and talk about some of the brave things that Floppy did when he was Superdog. Show them the words on the news stand and explain that these words are intended to remind them of Floppy's adventures. Ask the children to write a sentence about each of the other four things Floppy did. The words on the sheet should mean that they do not need to consult the story book and will be encouraged to form their own sentences.

Further activity: Ask the children to write two sentences to explain what happened when the adventure ended and Floppy was at home. They can use the back of the sheet for this activity. Remind them to check all the punctuation on their sheets.

Main learning outcome: to write simple evaluations of books read and discussed, giving reasons (T12)

Activity: These questions are intended to help children vary their responses to a story. They could be used in a group discussion before the children start to write or they could be used for children to read and respond to without any further explanation.

Further activity: ask the children to use the answers to the questions to write a book review using page 128 as a format.

Some words have the same spelling pattern but do not rhyme.
Find the word that does not rhyme with the other two. Write it
in the rectangle.

			Odd one out	rhymes with
1	year	fear	bear	bear	( )
2	come	gnome	some		( )
3	town	grown	down		( )
4	treat	great	heat		( )
5	does	goes	toes		( )
6	pull	bull	dull		( )
7	move	love	prove		( )
8	enough	rough	through		( )
9	thought	ought	drought		( )
10	though	cough	dough		( )

Now think of a word to rhyme with each word in the rectangle. Write it
in the oval.

bear   rhymes with    fair

Work
check

When Floppy was Superdog, he did five brave things.

1 Floppy saved a baby when he stopped a pram running down a hill.

Write a sentence about four more brave things Floppy did.
Use the words on the news stand to remind you.

2 ....

   ....

   ....

Superdog

handbag   docks
    thief   boy
shirt Hook Fang
  Snap   nasty
building girder
   dangerous
       rope

3 ....

   ....

   ....

4 ....

   ....

5 ....

   ....

Work check

Think about the story of <u>Superdog</u> and answer these questions.

Does <u>Superdog</u> remind you of another story?

The story of <u>Superdog</u> reminds me of

Did the story make you laugh?

I thought it was funny when

What was the bravest thing Floppy did?

I thought Floppy was brave when

Did you feel sorry for Floppy?

I felt sorry for Floppy when

Would you recommend this book to a friend?

I think you will like this story because

Work check

Main learning outcome: to reinforce work on discriminating syllables in reading and spelling from previous term (W2)

Activity: Provided that the children have done recent work on syllables, they should be able to read and respond to the sheet without further explanation. If they are not sure what to do, work through the first example with them. Look at page 3 and read the clue. It should be clear that the answer is 'sandwiches'. Ask the children to write one letter at a time on each of the dashes. The slash strokes divide the word into syllables. Help the children to read the word in three parts: 'sand/wich/es', then read the whole word normally.

Further activity: Ask the children to choose any four 2-syllable words from the story, e.g. litter, bleeding, broken. Tell them to write a clue, a page number and the syllable pattern for each word on the back of the sheet. They can swap their work with a friend to solve the puzzles.

Main learning outcome: the need for grammatical agreement, matching verbs to nouns/pronouns; using simple gender forms his/her correctly (S2)

Activity: Children should find this sheet self-explanatory. There are gaps in the story to be filled with words chosen from those in the brackets on each line. Remind the children to go back and read the whole paragraph to check that the words they have chosen make sense.

Further activity: Ask the children to find page 8 of the story. Tell them to copy out the page, on the back of the sheet, pretending that Floppy is a girl dog. They should be able to find five words that need to be changed.

Main learning outcome: to write sustained stories, using their knowledge of story elements, settings, characterization, dialogue and the language of story (T10)

Activity: Remind the children that Chip won a prize with his story of *The Litter Queen*. Read through Chip's ideas with the children. Ask them to think of a dream, nightmare or adventure about themselves. Show them how they can make notes to plan their story. Ask them to write their ideas in each box to create a story plan.

Further activity: Ask the children to use a copy of page 128 or a booklet they make for themselves to write the story in full. They will probably need time outside the Literacy Hour to complete their stories, particularly if they are going to illustrate them and present them to other children.

Look for words with three syllables or more. The clues will help you.
The letters must fit the number of dashes.

What tasted really good?
(p3)
__ __ __ __ / __ __ __ __ / __ __

How does litter make a place look?
(p5)
__ __ __ / __ __ / __ __ __

It looks like a flying chair.
(p7)
__ __ / __ __ __ / __ __ __ __ __

Broken bottles are this.
(p9)
__ __ __ / __ __ __ / __ __ __

When something happens quickly.
(p14)
__ __ __ / __ __ __ / __ __

The Litter Queen's palace was this.
(p16)
__ __ __ / __ __ / __ __ __

What Chip had to put on.
(p19)
__ / __ __ / __ __ __ __

Find these three-syllable words. Write a clue for each one.

(p22) __ __ __ __ / __ __ __ / __ __ __ __

....

(p32) __ __ / __ __ __ / __ __ __ __

....

Work
check

Write the missing words in the story.

They _____ the picnic things to the car, (take took taking)

then _____ walked to the top of the hill. (he they them)

Everyone _____ down for a rest. (sit sat sits)

Floppy _____ in and out of the trees. (ran run runs)

Suddenly _____ yelped. (he him his)

Floppy couldn't _____ properly. (walk walked walking)

_____ paw was bleeding. (Her His He)

Write the missing words in these sentences.

The children wanted to play cricket, so _____ had a

game before _____ went home. Floppy tried to join in,

but _____ couldn't because _____ paw was too sore.

At last, _____ was time to go home.

Thank-you for taking _____ ,' said the children.

Work
check

STAGE 9: *The Litter Queen*

Chip wrote a story about his adventure called 'The Litter Queen'.
Use his story plan to help you make up a story about a dream or an adventure.

	Chip's idea:	My idea:
The setting	The Litter Queen's palace. Litter and junk everywhere.	
The characters	I meet the Litter Queen who is bossy, cross. She has pet rats.	
Story plot	The Litter Queen makes me spread litter in lovely places.	
What happens next?	I have to go up in a microlight to drop litter over the countryside.	
The ending:	I fall out of the microlight and wake up in bed.	

Work check

Main learning outcome: to secure phonemic spelling (W1)

Further outcomes: new words linked to particular topics (W9)

Activity: Ask the children to read the beginning of Wilma's story again from pages 2 and 3. Then ask them to close the book and write the missing words on the sheet from memory. The first letter is included to help the children predict the right word. All the words have long vowel sounds or blends covered in the previous five terms. If an adult is available he or she will be able to discuss the children's suggestions for the missing words and show them how to re-read the text to check for meaning. Alternatively, the sheet can be used to assess children's ability to use context and an initial letter clue to choose and spell the right words.

Further activity: Ask the children to scan through the book, making a list of words used when someone speaks instead of 'said'. They should be able to find 'asked', 'thought', 'wondered', 'cried', 'shouted', 'squeaked', 'called', 'whispered' and 'hissed'. If time, they could look in other books too.

Main learning outcome: to use commas in lists (S4)

Further activity: to write in clear sentences using capital letters and full stops correctly (S5)

Activity: Ask the children to scan through the book to complete the lists. The first sentence asks them to find and list all the characters. Further lists should be self-explanatory but children will need a copy of the story each, or one between two if you want them to work in pairs.

Further activity: Ask the children to write four sentences about Wilma's adventures on the back of the sheet, e.g. 'Wilma fell in a swamp but a unicorn pulled her out.'

Main learning outcome: to write sustained stories, using their knowledge of story elements: narrative, settings, characterization, dialogue and the language of story (T10)

Activity: Ask the children to read each section of the plan, changing Wilma's ideas one by one to ideas of their own. When they have answered all the questions they should have a clear idea of the main points of their story. They should be able to give the group or the class an oral outline of their story from their notes.

Further activity: Using sheet 128 or a homemade storybook the children should be able to write an extended story of their own quest based on their notes. This may need to be completed outside the Literacy Hour.

Read pages 2 and 3 again. Close the book and write the missing words in the story.
Spell the words yourself.

L_____ ago and f_____ away, there was a

beautiful l_____ called Ulm. Flowers g_____

everywhere. Animals lived in the w_____ and forests.

Everyone was h_____ there. In a big cave d_____

underground, was the crystal bell of Ulm. It was

v_____ beautiful. Even in the d_____ cave, it

glowed like f_____ .

When it rang, its n_____ was l_____ music. The

s_____ of the bell t_____ every animal, every

plant and every t_____ when it was spring or

summer.

Write the words to match these pictures.

 _____

 _____

 _____

 _____

Write lists to complete these sentences.
Remember commas after each item but not
before 'and'!

The characters in Wilma's story are Grimlock, _____

_____

_____

The places Wilma visits in the land of Ulm are the forest, _____

_____

_____

In his bag the gnome was carrying a lemon, _____

_____

_____

When the bell returned to Ulm, beauty came to the land, birds _____

_____

_____

Work
check

STAGE 9: *The Quest*

Name _____ Date _____

Plan your own story of a quest.

	Wilma's idea:	My idea:
The beginning:	Long ago and far away, there was a beautiful land called Ulm.	
What is lost?	a crystal bell	
Who goes on the quest? (the hero or heroine)	a girl	
Who is the wicked person? (the villain)	Grimlock	
Who will help?	a unicorn and a a gnome	
Where is the special thing hidden?	Grimlock's castle in the mountains	
What has magic power?	a ring given by the unicorn	

Work
check

Main learning outcome: to secure phonemic spelling from previous five terms (W1); revision of *or* sound in phonemes *or, oor, aw, au*

Further outcomes: revision of *er* sound in *er, ur, ir* (W1)

Activity: Ask children to look in the wordsearch puzzle for words with *or* sounds and *or, oor, aw* and *au* spellings. Tell them to circle each word then write it in the correct box at the bottom of the page. Ask the children which phoneme is used most often. Suggest they add one more word to each box if they can.

Further activity: Tell the children to look at the wordsearch again, this time for words written downwards. Ask them to make a list on the back of the sheet. They should write the words again in lists with the same phonemic spellings. (There are seven words in the puzzle: survival, surf, fur, were, her, girl and bird.) Ask the children to add more words with *ur, er* and *ir* phonemes, helping each other in pairs or in a group.

Main learning outcome: the need for grammatical agreement using simple gender forms correctly, e.g. his, her (S2)

Further outcome: to write using capital letters and full stops (S5)

Activity: Ask children to choose 'his', 'her' or 'their' to fill the gaps in the story. Remind them to read on past the gap before deciding which word is best. When they have completed the sheet the children should read the whole story again to make sure it makes sense.

Further activity: On the back of the sheet, ask the children to make up three more sentences about the story using 'his', 'her' and 'their'. (One sentence for each word.)

Main learning outcome: to understand the distinction between fact and fiction; to use the terms 'fact' and 'fiction' appropriately (T13)

Activity: The children should be able to read and respond to the instructions without further explanation. If anyone is unsure what to do, ask them to read each sentence and decide whether it is a true statement (a fact), or imagined by the author for the story (fiction). At the bottom of the page children are asked to write one more fact that can be taken from the story, e.g. 'You can catch fish in rivers.' When they have finished they can compare their answers with a partner and justify their decisions.

Further activity: Ask the children to write three more sentences about the story on the back of the sheet. The sentences can be fact or fiction. At the end of the lesson ask the group whether each one is fact or fiction.

Find words with **or**, **oor**, **aw** and **au** phonemes in this puzzle.

t	o	r	c	h	s	t	o	r	e
p	a	w	d	o	c	t	o	r	s
k	s	a	w	n	b	f	o	r	u
m	o	r	e	m	i	r	r	o	r
s	h	o	r	e	r	l	a	w	v
u	e	m	e	g	d	o	o	r	i
r	r	s	t	i	d	r	a	w	v
f	l	o	o	r	s	o	r	e	a
u	t	r	c	l	a	w	o	r	l
r	a	w	b	c	a	u	g	h	t

List the words here.

or	
oor	
aw	
au	

There are most words in the ⬚ box.

Fill the gaps in these sentences with **his**, **her** or **their**.

Amy and her family were on a journey but _____ wagons were stuck in the mud.

Amy left _____ family and went for a walk.

She couldn't find _____ way back. She got _____ foot stuck in a trap.

Little Fox was out on _____ own.

He was a long way from _____ village.

A bear heard Amy shouting. He stood on _____ hind legs and sniffed the air.

The bear ran towards them. Biff opened _____ umbrella and spun it round.

The bear had never seen anything like it in _____ life. He ran away.

The children told Little Fox's father about _____ adventure in the wood.

Amy told him about _____ mother and father.

In the morning he took Amy to _____ wagon train.

Work
check

STAGE 9: *Survival Adventure*

Decide whether these sentences are true (fact) or were made up for the story (fiction).

Write **fact** or **fiction** in each box.

The children were pulled into a new adventure.

People used to travel in wagons.

Trappers used metal traps to catch animals.

Little Fox found Amy caught in the trap.

The magic took Biff, Chip and Wilf to the woods.

Biff and Little Fox smashed the trap.

Bears are not very friendly.

You can make a fire without matches.

It is easy to get lost in the woods.

The children watched the wagon train for
a long time.

Write one more fact from the story here.

Work
check

Checklist of high frequency words for years 1 and 2 (pages 124 and 125)

Main learning outcome: to read on sight and spell all the words from Appendix List 1 (W4)

Activity: This list is reproduced in alphabetical order as a checklist. You could use it either as an individual assessment and record to show how many words the child is able to read and spell confidently; or, at the end of Year 1 or the end of Key Stage 1, to pass on as a record to the next teacher; or to cut up and send home as revision spelling lists; or to enlarge and display as a reference for the spelling of high frequency words.

Stages 8 and 9 high frequency words (pages 126 and 127)

Main learning outcome: to read on sight high frequency words likely to occur in graded texts (W5) As there are no lists of key words at Stages 8 and 9, six words have been selected for each story to use to check that the child's sight vocabulary is increasing.

Activity: These lists can be used as assessments in the same way as the words from Appendix List 1 and as a means of deciding which book the child should move on to next. Where words from Appendix List 2 are common within the story, these words have been chosen.

Story format (page 128)

Main learning outcome: to write sustained stories, using their knowledge of story elements (T10); to apply phonological, graphic knowledge and sight vocabulary to spell words accurately (T9)

Activity: This sheet can be used as a format for story writing after an introductory discussion or after using planning sheets on pages 94, 114 and 118. The story can be used to assess the child's ability to create a coherent story with some of the above elements and to assess the child's approach to spelling unknown words.

about	did	home	new
after	do	house	next
again	don't	how	night
an	dig	if	not
another	door	jump	now
as	down	just	off
back	first	last	old
ball	from	laugh	once
be	girl	little	one
because	good	live(d)	or
bed	got	love	our
been	had	made	out
boy	half	make	over
brother	has	man	people
but	have	many	push
by	help	may	pull
call(ed)	her	more	put
came	here	much	ran
can't	him	must	saw
could	his	name	school

seen	very	one	January
should	want	two	February
sister	water	three	March
so	way	four	April
some	were	five	May
take	when	six	June
than	what	seven	July
hat	where	eight	August
their	who	nine	September
hem	will	ten	October
hen	with	eleven	November
here	would	twelve	December
hese	your	thirteen	red
hree	Monday	fourteen	orange
ime	Tuesday	fifteen	yellow
oo	Wednesday	sixteen	green
ook	Thursday	seventeen	blue
ee	Friday	eighteen	indigo
vo	Saturday	nineteen	violet
s	Sunday	twenty	black

The Kidnappers

because   busy   together

sure   many   laughed

Viking Adventure

under   never   animals

along   believe   light

The Rainbow Machine

after   across   sometimes

young   thought   heavy

The Flying Carpet

please   already   better

towards   safe   thank you

A Day in London

somewhere   window   around

excited   these   second

Victorian Adventure

great   money   washed

night   trouble   important

Work check

Green Island

island square feathers

caught famous newspaper

Storm Castle

computer exciting danger

much friendly numbers

Superdog

television swimming anyway

someone rescue minute

The Litter Queen

country behind strange

afraid competition special

The Quest

write journey beautiful

worse secret noise

Survival Adventure

listen easy morning

trouble father without

Work
check

Name

Date

T10 Writing stories

fold